C000026582

THE BEATLES

THE BAND THAT CHANGED THE WORLD

TERRY BURROWS

CARLTON
BOOKS

THIS IS A CARLTON BOOK

Published by Carlton Books Limited
20 Mortimer Street
London W1T 3JW

A CIP catalogue for this book is available from the British Library.

ISBN 978-1-78097-929-8

Editorial: Charlotte Selby
Design: Russell Knowles and James Pople
Picture Research: Steve Behan
Production: Lisa Hedicker

Printed in Dubai

10 9 8 7 6 5 4 3 2 1

CONTENTS

INTRODUCTION

Saturday July 6, 1957 is not a date that would evoke strong memories for many people. In the city of Liverpool it was probably much the same as any other summer's day. School was out until the end of August, so the city and the suburbs would have been littered with bored teenagers looking for adventure or mischief. They might have been hanging about in coffee bars feeding the jukebox. They probably *wouldn't* have been listening to the radio – all they would have heard there was the dull drone of light orchestral music and middle-aged crooners. It would have been just like any other day.

John Lennon, a 17-year-old art school student, had found his own solution – rock 'n' roll. His group, The Quarry Men, played wherever and whenever they could find an audience. Today, though, he failed to notice that someone in the typically small crowd was watching his performance more intently than anyone else. After the show, his friend Ivan Vaughan told him there was someone he'd like him to meet. Paul McCartney stepped forward. Saturday July 6, 1957 was indeed a historic date in the annals of popular music.

The mid-1950s had seen the start of a revolution imported from across the Atlantic that would forever divide generations: the cult of youth. With the advent of rock 'n' roll, the first teenagers were born. To Lennon and McCartney, and a million others like them, Elvis Presley had saved the world from terminal mediocrity. Their lives had been given new meaning. But with a new decade dawning, things seemed to be drifting backwards: Elvis had been drafted into the US Army, and his career had been put on hold; and the hugely popular and influential Buddy Holly was dead. Sure, there were new stars, but these were merely a new generation of clean-cut, all-American crooners or – worse still – feeble British imitations. It was beginning to look as if those wishful thinkers who had doubted rock 'n' roll's longevity might have been right – perhaps it had all just been a passing fad. But it was too late for Lennon and McCartney. They'd caught the fever and there would be no going back.

When The Beatles' debut single, "Love Me Do", gently crept into the UK Top 20 near the end of 1962, most people thought they were just another new group – an overnight sensation. Few knew of the years they had devoted to learning their craft or the seven-hour performances in seedy nightclubs on Hamburg's Reeperbahn, which had turned them into polished performers. And nobody could have predicted that popular culture was about to be blown apart, and that pretty much everything The Beatles would create over the next seven years, not only their music, but their clothes, their haircuts, their behaviour, their album sleeves and their attitudes would effectively define an era.

Think of the key events of the decade, from John F. Kennedy's assassination to Neil Armstrong setting foot on the moon. Now start filling in the gaps: "Beatlemania"; The Beatles on *The Ed Sullivan Show*; The Royal Variety Performance; The MBEs; the "more popular than Jesus" controversy; "Yellow Submarine"; *Sgt. Pepper*; "All You Need Is Love" broadcast via the first worldwide satellite link; the Maharishi; the "bed-ins"; the drug busts ... the list seems endless. Right up to their miserable demise in 1970, the fortunes and activities in The Beatles camp mirrored the path of an entire decade. For many people – and some who were not yet born – the 1960s were such special years because they were touched by the genius of The Beatles.

The influence The Beatles had on the course of popular music was, clearly, profound – indeed it is incalculable. That influence has continued to make its presence felt in the gap left by their parting. Pretty much every major songwriter of the past four decades will have cited Lennon and McCartney as a source of inspiration. Producers point to the collaboration between The Beatles and George Martin as benchmarks in the use of the recording studio. Some have gone a whole lot further, successive generations producing their own "*faux* Beatles" – from the Electric Light Orchestra in the 1970s and 1980s to Oasis, one of the most popular bands of the 1990s.

Living in an age where the old divisions of high and low culture have largely been demolished, it comes as no surprise to see The Beatles afforded as much respect as the greatest composers or jazz musicians. What is surprising is how much they have become a part of our lives. Although over 40 years have passed since they made their final recordings, The Beatles remain to this day the most famous pop group of them all.

Terry Burrows, London

JOHN LENNON

WORKING-CLASS HERO

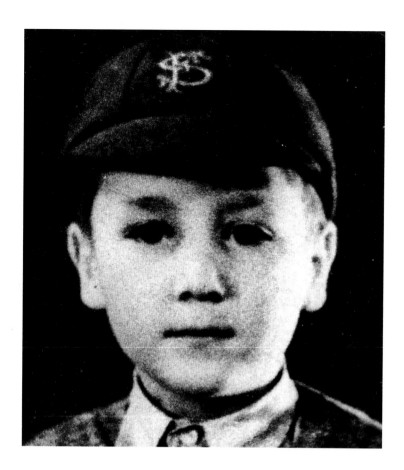

The city of Liverpool was the principal port in the north-west of England, and one of Europe's traditional seafaring gateways to America. That meant it wasn't the safest place to be living in the early days of the Second World War. October 9, 1940 saw a particularly fierce spate of night raids, but this was the last thing on the young Julia Lennon's mind as she lay in Liverpool's Oxford Street Maternity Hospital. With bombs falling around the hospital, Julia gave birth to a boy. She decided to name him John. His second name, in honour of Britain's wartime prime minister, was Winston.

Julia was one of five daughters. Her father worked for The Liverpool & Glasgow Salvage Association – the numerous shipwrecks along The Mersey had kept him and his colleagues busy ever since the first air raids began. Julia was the wild one of the family. Two years earlier, she'd married long-time sweetheart Alf "Freddy" Lennon, at least partly to defy the wishes of her father. It was not to be the closest of relationships: Freddy worked on the great passenger liners that travelled between Liverpool and New York and they were apart more often than not.

Freddy was berthed in New York when war broke out. Wanting to avoid participation at all costs, he jumped ship. He was eventually interned at Ellis Island, and ended up serving a sentence for desertion at a British military prison in North Africa. Julia herself would later admit that her decision to marry Freddy was one of the least serious of her life. While Freddy returned to Liverpool for a few brief visits in 1940, he largely disappeared from her life from that year onwards. Freddy did reappear briefly in 1945 and tried to persuade Julia and John to move to New Zealand with him. When Julia refused, John was given the option of choosing between his two parents. It would be a long time before he was to see his father again.

JULIA

Julia Stanley was born on March 12, 1914, the daughter of George and Annie Stanley. She was the fourth of five children, all girls, and had a reputation for being impulsive, flighty and funny. She was also musically talented, as was her mostly absent husband, Alf "Freddy" Lennon. Their only child together, John, was her first, but she went on to have three daughters – the first of whom she put up for adoption, under pressure.

Although John spent most of his childhood living with his aunts, especially Mimi, Julia remained close to him, keeping in very regular contact. She strongly encouraged his musical and free-spirited tendencies, and, despite Mimi's significant disapproval, bought him his first guitar. During his teenage years, John would often stay at the house Julia shared with Bobby Dykins and their two daughters, Julia and Jacqui.

Tragically, Julia was killed on July 15, 1958 by a drunk learner-driver, an off-duty policeman named Eric Clague. Drinking and driving was not illegal at that time, and Clague's testimony stated that she simply walked out of the hedge-lined central reservation straight in front of him. He was acquitted of all charges.

Julia was buried in Liverpool's Allerton Cemetery.

The war brought hardship to everyone, but it was an especially difficult time for a young mother. Julia was not only unhappy but unsettled too. Much of the burden of childcare fell on other members of her family. During this time it gradually became apparent that her sister Mimi was forming an especially close relationship with John. Far from causing any jealousy, Julia was relieved. Julia was young and attractive and soon there was a new man in her life. Working at a café in Penny Lane, she met John "Bobby" Dykins and fell in love.

Julia agreed to let John live with the childless Mimi and her husband George Smith. She hoped this would provide him with a more stable environment. He moved to Mendips, a semi-detached house in Menlove Avenue, Woolton, a pleasant middle-class suburb three miles outside Liverpool's city centre. Julia knew that her son would be well looked after and that she would still see him most days.

John's artistic leanings emerged from birth. He was a bright child who had easily learned to read by the age of four. Mimi sent him off to school at Dovedale Primary, near Penny Lane. One of John's earliest passions was reading. He soon developed an interest in writing and drawing his own books and comics. He also began to develop a taste for the kind of petty mischief that would get him into trouble in the future.

At the age of 12 John was sent up to Quarry Bank Grammar, a school with a fine record of academic achievement. He started out as one of the school's brightest hopes, but with his friend Pete Shotton always close at hand, John began a startling academic decline, increasingly creating trouble. Mimi, by now a widow, began to dread the phone calls from the school secretary detailing her charge's latest petty misdemeanours. By his early teens, John Lennon had already carved out a reputation as a rebel.

While John worshipped Aunt Mimi, he had always remained very close to his mother. As he grew older he began to see more and more of her, often cutting classes to do so. He thought of Julia more as an older sister than his mother. What's more, she told him the kind of things that he wanted to hear, such as not to worry about homework or what might happen in the future. This was in total contrast to Aunt Mimi, who was something of a disciplinarian.

Previous spread: Johm Lennon pictured backstage wearing a pinstripe jacket in England, 1964.

Opposite above: Headshot portrait of John as a young boy in a school uniform and cap, c. 1948.

Opposite below: The young John Lennon in Liverpool with his mother, Julia Stanley.

Right: Post-Beatles John Lennon, shortly before the release of his hugely successful solo album, *Imagine*, 1971.

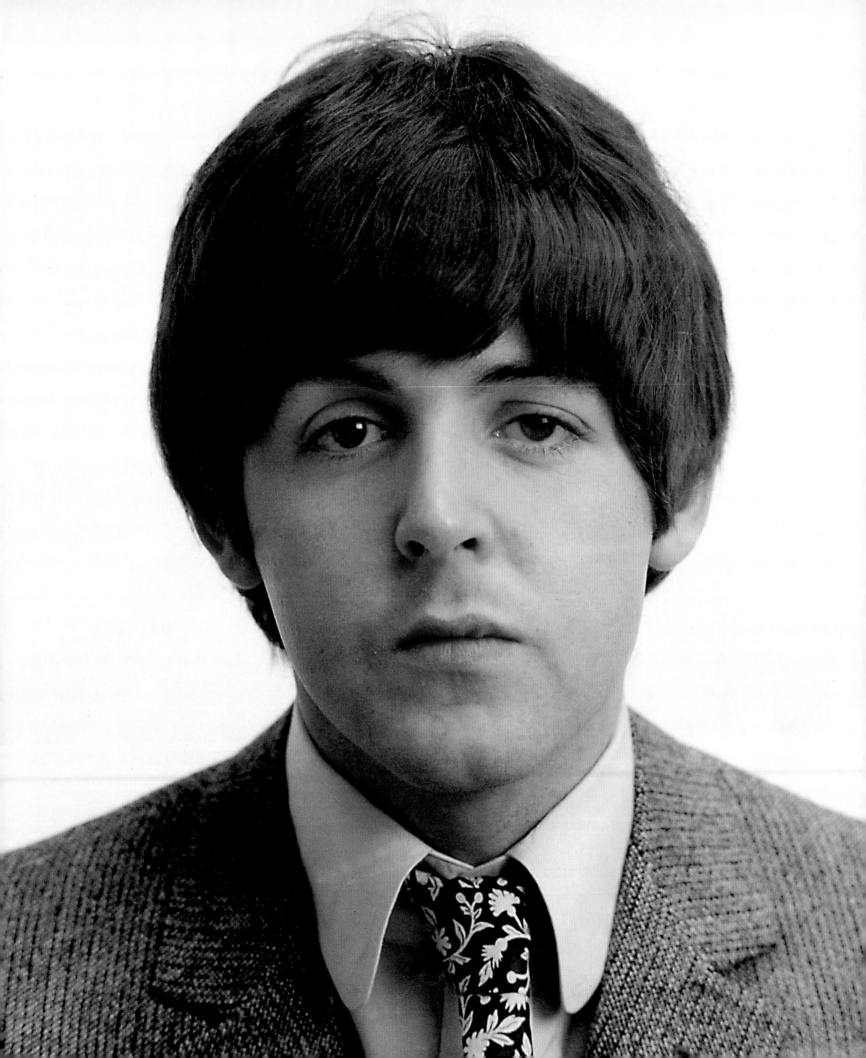

PAUL McCARTNEY

MUSIC IN THE GENES

James Paul McCartney was born in Liverpool's Walton General Hospital on June 18, 1942. His father Jim, like many "Scousers", had an Irish background. He worked during the day on the Liverpool Cotton Exchange in Chapel Street, before the war forced its closure. At night, however, he turned to his first love – music. Jim was a self-taught pianist who led the Jim Mac Jazz Band, making a few extra shillings playing at social clubs and works dances. While Jim McCartney had a reputation as a diligent and skilful salesman, he was also by all accounts something of ladies' man. Having successfully escaped the responsibility of marriage and a family throughout his twenties and thirties, he seemed destined for a life of bachelorhood. Then he met Mary Mohan. They married in 1941, a few months before Jim's 40th birthday.

Paul was seemingly graced from birth with charm that would get him out of all manner of childhood scrapes. Performing well at primary school, he easily passed his Eleven plus examination, winning a place at the City's most prestigious grammar school, The Liverpool Institute. He was a model pupil, always helpful and quietly studious.

Paul's grandfather, Joe McCartney, was strictly traditional about his musical tastes. He had always been hopeful of interesting his children in the musical arts. Jim irritated his father by turning to ragtime music at the age of 17,

having learnt to play both the piano and the trumpet by ear. Joe had little time for Jim's choice of musical style, but that didn't stop Paul's father. Jim first appeared in public with a band called the Masked Melody Makers, who were remembered for wearing black masks on stage. His first composition was a song called "Eloise", to which Paul would later add lyrics and, as a tribute to his father, record in the mid-1970s as "Walking in the Park with Eloise".

In 1955, when Paul was still only 13, his mother fell ill. After experiencing pains in her chest she was diagnosed as having breast cancer. By the time she was taken into hospital for exploratory surgery, the cancer had already spread too far and the proposed mastectomy operation could not be performed. Mary died shortly afterwards. Devastated by the loss, Jim took over the arduous task of managing the family finances alone.

With a musician for a father, the McCartney household had always been filled with music. Like many homes before the arrival of television, the family's upright piano – purchased coincidentally from Brian Epstein's father, Harry, at the NEMS shop – was the centrepiece around which everyone would congregate for communal sing-songs. But the McCartneys were now distinctly out of tune with each other. Jim had already bought a nickel-plated trumpet for Paul's birthday following Mary's death. Like John Lennon, however, Paul had

THE McCARTNEY ROOTS

The last native Irish member of the McCartney line was James, Paul's great-great-grandfather. He moved from Ireland to Scotland in around 1860, with James II already a growing lad. The family then moved on, eventually settling in Liverpool. James II was a painter and plumber, and although they were both under age, he married one Elizabeth Williams in 1864. Their son Joseph was born on November 23, 1866 and became a worker in a tobacco plant. He married Florrie Cleg in 1896. They were a well-respected couple: Joe never drank or swore, and was always in bed by 10 p.m., while Florrie was known as the local agony aunt, and was referred to by all and sundry as "Granny Mac". Paul's father Jim was born July 7, 1902, the third of seven children, and grew up in Everton, less than a mile from Liverpool city centre.

Owen Mohin, Mary's father, was born in 1880 in Tullynamalrow in County Monaghan, Ireland. He slightly altered his surname in school, from Mohin to Mohan, because there were so many other students sharing the Mohin name. Owen became a coalman when he moved to Liverpool, and in 1905 he married Mary Danher of Toxteth. Paul's mother Mary was born on September 29, 1909 in Fazakerley, Liverpool. She was only 11 years old when her mother died in childbirth. When her father remarried, Mary went to live with a succession of aunts, before training as a nurse at Alder Hey hospital at the age of 14. She eventually became a ward sister at Walton General Hospital, and then a health visitor and midwife.

also heard Lonnie Donegan and wanted to play a guitar. While Jim McCartney had displayed an interest in the new rock 'n' roll music, he was more concerned that his family should not have a Teddy Boy in their number. He was also largely unconvinced of the merits of the guitar as a musical instrument.

Eventually, without too much persuasion – and quite possibly remembering his own childhood and his musical disagreements with his father – Jim relented. One day he took the trumpet out with him to work, and came home having exchanged it for a sunburst-coloured guitar. He set about teaching Paul some basic chords. However, he was surprised to see the difficulty his son experienced in squeezing the fingers of his left hand into position on the fret board. Paul struggled for a while before giving up completely. Until, that is, the day he discovered that by holding the guitar in the other hand the whole process was somehow much simpler. This was rather strange: while Paul McCartney was right-handed in every other way, for some mysterious reason, playing the guitar right-handed felt completely wrong. After restringing the guitar, he once again set about learning the chords. This time there was no turning back.

From that moment on, Paul devoted all his waking hours to the instrument, and – like generations of others before and since – a promising start to an academic career was cut short by the lure of the six-stringed beast.

Previous spread: Posed studio session of Paul McCartney, 1965.

Opposite: Paul with father, Jim, and elder brother Mike – who would himself later find fame with The Scaffold.

Right: The bowler-hatted model of respectability would have to wait until 1997 to receive his knighthood.

GEORGE HARRISON

THE DARK HORSE

George Harrison was born on February 24, 1943. (It was assumed for years that he was born on February 25 but it was later discovered he was born just before midnight on February 24). His father Harry had originally been a steward on a passenger ship, but lost his job during the Depression. He now worked for Liverpool Corporation as a bus conductor. George's mother Louise had worked in a greengrocer's shop before starting a family. Compared to John or Paul, George's Liverpool upbringing was a much earthier affair.

George Harrison was the youngest of four children – three boys and a girl. The eldest, his sister Louise, was almost 12 years older than he was, and one of his brothers, Harry, was eight years older. The other brother, Peter, was closer to his age, having been born in July 1940. Even so, George was definitely the baby of the household. His parents were both Liverpudlians born and bred. Louise, his mother, came from a partly Irish background, as her father, John French, had moved to Liverpool from County Wexford in Ireland. Once in

Liverpool, French married a local woman. George's father, Harry Harrison, was a former steward for the White Star Line, and had gone on to work on the buses.

At the time of George's birth, the family lived in very modest conditions in a small terraced home in Liverpool's Wavertree district. Number 12 Arnold Grove had an outside lavatory, with one coal fireplace as the sole source of heating, and it backed on to an alleyway. The Harrisons were finally offered council housing when George was seven, and moved from Wavertree to Speke with what must have been a certain amount of relief.

George's early education took place at the same school as John Lennon – Dovedale Primary. The two had no specific contact however, because George, being much younger, was in a different school year. In 1954, George won a place at the Liverpool Institute, the same grammar school that Paul McCartney attended. His school career, however, was destined to go nowhere and at a great speed.

George quickly developed a hatred for all kinds of formal teaching. Unlike Lennon, he didn't cause trouble or make a nuisance of himself. He rebelled quietly, simply refusing to take part in school life. By the age of 13, he had found solace in the guitar and skiffle music. George borrowed the money from his mother to buy a good guitar – one with a cutaway at the top of the body. He paid off the debt by taking a Saturday morning delivery round at his local butcher's shop. Around this time, George formed a skiffle band named the Rebels. This was really the only pursuit that he cared about. With George in the Rebels and Paul McCartney in The Quarry Men, and both schoolboys being more interested in rock 'n' roll than school, it's no real surprise that the two met and became friends.

Despite being keen to join Paul in The Quarry Men, of which John Lennon was also a member, George was initially kept out due to his age. That didn't stop him hanging around the group however, and because he was always available to fill a gap, he did get to play with them occasionally. He gradually became an accepted member, and by the time he reached the age of 16, George Harrison was a fully-fledged Quarry Man – albeit one who was still treated as the baby of the band (a role that would haunt him throughout his entire career with The Beatles).

School had been of total disinterest to George for years, and he quietly left at around the same time as he finally cemented his place in the band. He found an apprenticeship as an electrician at one of the Liverpool department stores, Blacklers. This fell by the wayside when The Beatles were offered their first stint in Germany in August 1960. George continued taking his guitar-playing seriously, however, using the gruelling Hamburg sets to hone his skills, getting further instruction from early Beatles' collaborator Tony Sheridan at The Indra club. Although George's youth proved the start of the band's deportation debacle during that first Hamburg stint, no one blamed him for any of the subsequent hassle.

THE LIVERPOOL INSTITUTE

The Liverpool Mechanics' School of Arts was established in 1825. Like many other similar establishments of that time, it was founded to provide evening education to working men and to offer casual lectures to the general public on topics ranging from evolution to Shakespeare's plays. In 1832, its name was shortened to The Liverpool Mechanics' Institution, and by 1840 it was also offering day school services to boys. It then opened a girls' school across the road in 1844, one of the first public girls' schools in the UK. By the early 1850s, the Institution's evening art classes had become so important that it was developing into an art school in its own right. In 1856, the name changed again to reflect this, to The Liverpool Institute and School of Art.

Over the next century, the Liverpool Institute developed a strong reputation as an excellent seat of learning, with hundreds of students going on to scholarships at the prestigious Oxford and Cambridge universities. Governors decided to donate the school and its assets to the City of Liverpool in 1905, and it became the cornerstone of Liverpool's city education system. It was renamed The Liverpool Institute High School for Boys, and remained the jewel in Liverpool's academic crown until the fall of selective schooling – the grammar school system – in the late 1960s.

The Liverpool Institute closed in 1985 after 20 years of neglect. Paul McCartney was horrified. Meanwhile, Beatles' producer George Martin knew that his acquaintance Mark Featherstone-Witty had been inspired by the 1980 movie Fame, and wanted to set up a British version of the New York High School for the Performing Arts. He put the two in touch, and after seven years of hard wrangling on Featherstone-Witty's part and a good deal of McCartney's money, the building re-opened as The Liverpool Institute for the Performing Arts in 1996. Its graduates include prominent US rocker Liam Lynch, TV presenter Dawn Porter and Hollyoaks star Leah Hackett.

Previous spread: George Harrison posing for a studio photograph, 1965.

Opposite: George Harrison and a woman from The Beatles' management company, NEMS, sort through his mountain of birthday cards from fans.

Right: George practising the acoustic guitar in Liverpool, circa 1954.

RINGO STARR

FINAL
PIECE OF
THE
PUZZLE

Richard Starkey (senior) and Elsie Gleave met while working for a baker in Liverpool. By the time they were married in 1936, Richard had begun working on the docks. They lived in a large terraced house in the Dingle, a poor, working-class area. Ringo Starr was born as Richard Starkey Jr on July 7, 1940. His parents' marriage lasted just seven years, with Richard leaving Elsie with little Ritchie in 1943. She moved to a smaller house in the same area and took work as a barmaid.

Ritchie's education seemed to be doomed from the start. He first attended St Silas primary school at the age of five. His schooling was interrupted a year later, when a burst appendix led to peritonitis, followed by a coma. He wasn't expected to survive. Ritchie regained consciousness after ten weeks, however, and began a slow recovery. One of the presents he was given to keep himself entertained was a drum, which greatly captured his imagination. Six months later, still in hospital, he knocked himself unconscious when he fell out of bed, setting his recovery back further. By the time he finally came home from hospital, Ritchie had been in there for more than a year.

Having lost so much time, Ritchie had fallen badly behind in his schooling and was placed in a class with much younger children. One of his neighbour's children, a girl named Marie Maguire, taught him how to read and write so that he could start to catch up. Even with her help, though, Ritchie had little interest in school and soon started to skip classes. These youthful excursions led to an unusually early alcohol problem, suffering blackouts by the age of nine. His schooling never fully recovered – so poor was his work that he wasn't even given the opportunity to sit for the Eleven Plus examinations.

Ritchie was enthusiastic about Elsie's second marriage, to house-painter Harry Graves in 1953 – she won him over by being supportive of his musical interests. He and Graves became close, and Ritchie used to jokingly refer to the man as his "step-ladder". After a couple of abortive attempts at finding work, Ritchie became an apprentice joiner at an engineering firm. Along with Eddie Miles, a fellow apprentice, he started a skiffle group. Along with some other colleagues, they used to entertain the rest of the staff at lunchtimes – Ritchie naturally handling percussion.

For Christmas 1957, Harry Graves bought Ritchie a drum kit in London, lugging it all the way back up to Liverpool on the train. It was a ramshackle second-hand affair, but from that point on it was inevitable that the quiet lad who'd turned to drumming for solace so often in the past would try to make a living as a professional drummer.

Ritchie spent some time playing with the Darktown Skiffle Group, and often sat in with other bands, including, in March 1959, a group called Al Caldwell's Texans. Six months later, he joined the Texans officially. By this time they were calling themselves Rory Storm and the Hurricanes. The band dressed outrageously, put on a boisterous stage show, and quickly established themselves as one of Liverpool's top bands. When they were offered a three-month Summer booking to play at the Butlins holiday camp in Pwllheli in North Wales, Ritchie finally had to choose between his apprenticeship – and his fiancée at the time, a girl called Geraldine – and the lure of rock 'n' roll – not to mention an impressive £20 per week. Despite everything his parents, employers and girlfriend could say, music won over.

Vocalist Rory Storm had officially changed his name from Alan Caldwell by Deed Poll. He suggested to Ritchie that he should get a stage name for himself. Ritchie was already well-known in the group for wearing rings on every finger, and it wasn't long before Ritchie became "Rings", and then "Ringo". Starkey was then shortened to "Starr" so that his solo spots could be called "Starr Time". Like Rory, Ringo adopted his new name legally.

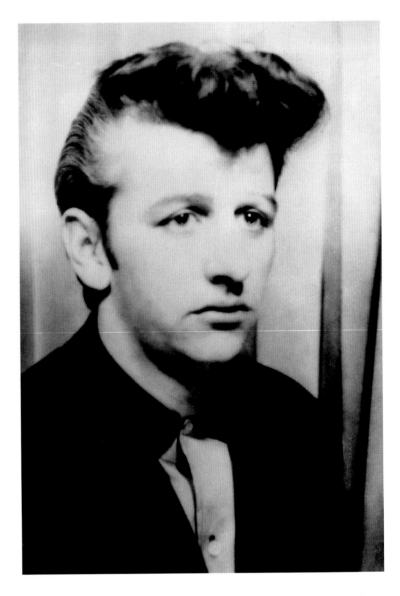

Rory Storm and the Hurricanes made the lead billing at the Hamburg Kaiserkeller in November 1960, where Ringo first met The Beatles. In 1961, Rory's group completed a tour of American air bases in France, another summer at Butlins, and then a series of local rounds in Liverpool. Ringo began to tire of the band's stagnation, and even thought seriously about immigrating to America to work in a factory in Texas. Instead he went back to Hamburg again in 1962, playing for Tony Sheridan, before rejoining Rory Storm for yet another Butlins summer season. He was already considering an offer from Kingsize Taylor and the Dominos when The Beatles made contact in August 1962. He would soon be the most famous drummer in the world.

Previous spread: Ringo Starr backstage while on tour with The Beatles in the UK, 1963.

Above: Ringo poses with his pompadour hairstyle while a member of Rory Storm and the Hurricanes, circa 1959.

Opposite above: Ringo with Rory Storm and the Hurricanes at a Butlin's holiday camp, circa 1962.

Opposite below: Ringo Starr on stage with the band at The Jive Hive, Liverpool, August 1963.

A QUIET TIME

The same year as Elsie married Harry, Ritchie caught a cold, which turned into pleurisy (an infection of the lining surrounding the lungs), and then tuberculosis. This led to a further two years in a sanatorium, a specialist hospital designed for lengthy recoveries.

As Starr says: "In those days, they used to put you in what we liked to call a greenhouse in the country – the countryside. And thank God someone had invented Streptomycin. And you just sat around for a year getting well … so, to keep you entertained, once a week, they'd have like lessons … could be knitting, could be modelling, occasionally it was music. And they'd bring in tambourines, triangles and little drums … [drums] became the dream that one day I would have my own set, which happened. And then the other dream was that I would play with other musicians, which came true."

1957–
1960

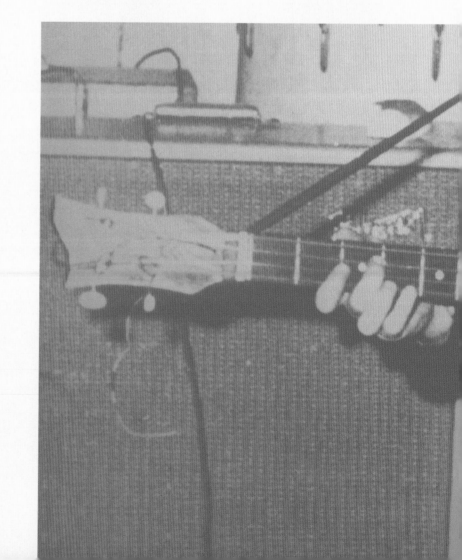

FROM
LIVERPOOL
TO
HAMBURG

BY THE TIME JOHN LENNON HAD REACHED HIS MID-TEENS, ROCK 'N' ROLL MUSIC IMPORTED FROM AMERICA WAS ALL THE RAGE. JOHN NOT ONLY LOVED THE MUSIC, BUT ALSO THE LOOK OF THE BRITISH ROCK 'N' ROLL FANS – THE NOTORIOUS TEDDY BOYS. WITH THEIR OUTLANDISH DRAPED JACKETS, FRILLED SHIRTS, SKIN-TIGHT "DRAINPIPE" TROUSERS, GREASED LOCKS AND QUIFFS FLOPPING DOWN OVER THE FOREHEAD, THE "TEDS" BECAME THE SCOURGE OF BRITAIN'S RESPECTABLE CITIZENRY. JOHN WOULD NOW TAKE EVERY OPPORTUNITY TO BEG AUNT MIMI OR JULIA TO BUY HIM THE CLOTHES.

But it was skiffle – a blues folk music that emerged in the United States in the early part of the 20th century – that first suggested to John the idea of creating his own music. British musician Lonnie Donegan's 1954 hit "Rock Island Line", featuring an acoustic guitar and washboard rhythm, created a short-lived skiffle craze that saw a host of groups springing up across the country. It was his mother who lent him the five pounds and ten shillings to buy his first guitar – a cheap Gallotone Spanish acoustic. From that moment, Lennon became convinced of his future. Mimi, however, was less convinced: "The guitar's all very well, John, but you'll never make a living out of it."

Mustering all the enthusiasm that they'd increasingly failed to put into their school work, John and Pete Shotton, Quarry Bank's own resident teenage rebels, decided to form their own skiffle group – The Quarry Men. With John singing and playing guitar, The Quarry Men were booked at school dances and youth clubs, playing a mix of Lonnie Donegan's songs and American rock 'n' roll hits.

John's school work continued to deteriorate to the point where he was now unlikely to pass any exams at all. However, breathing space arrived in the form of a young headmaster at Quarry Bank, who used his personal connections to arrange a place for John at the local art school.

"THIS IS PAUL. THIS IS JOHN."

The Quarry Men stumbled along, fired mostly by John's enthusiasm. On July 6, 1957, the band was booked to appear at the St Peter's Parish annual church fete in Woolton, where they were to play on the back of a lorry in the parade, and then afterwards on a small outdoor stage. John's friend Ivan Vaughan, an earlier member of The Quarry Men, attended the fete and brought along a school friend from the "posh" Liverpool Institute. He was especially keen for John to meet his friend and felt sure they would hit it off.

That friend was Paul McCartney and as The Quarry Men played their set, Paul watched intently from the side of the stage.

The first meeting between John and Paul was a decidedly cool affair. A few diffident greetings were tossed about until Paul revealed his winning secret: he knew how to tune a guitar properly. John's attitude softened further when Paul revealed that he knew *all* the words to a large number of rock 'n' roll songs. John had recently taken to making up his own lyrics – although this was primarily because he could never remember other people's all the way through. The meeting ended with Paul playing a brief set of Little Richard songs while John carefully studied the chord shapes he was playing.

Having Paul on the scene posed a dilemma for John as the group The Quarry Men had been an extension of his school gang and he was the undisputed leader of both. Paul would be a major asset to the group, but he was clearly a far better musician than any of the other members too. He also possessed a cocky arrogance and John realized that he wouldn't be able to boss him about in the same way as he did the others. Nonetheless, they began to spend more and more time together and while two more different personalities could hardly have been imagined – John, rebellious with his dry cutting wit, and Paul, ambitious and hard-working with an eagerness to please – their shared love of music and guitars brought them close together.

Previous spread: Paul on stage at the Cavern Club in Liverpool during the early days of The Beatles, circa 1960.

Right: The Fab Three standing outside Paul's home in Liverpool, circa 1960. Ringo was not to join the band until 1962.

THE FAB THREE

1958 would be a difficult year for John Lennon. At Liverpool College of Art he found himself surrounded by jazz-loving art students who despised the Teddy Boy in their midst and, as a result, he made few friends.

But matters took a tragic turn when Julia Lennon was knocked over by a car and killed in July. John was devastated. Unlike Mimi, Julia had been totally indulgent of his moods and attitudes and he, in turn, saw her as a carefree spirit, someone who without question would approve of anything he did. Although he always considered Mimi and George to be his "parents", Julia's sudden death left a gaping hole that would affect him throughout the rest of his life.

Things were also far from smooth in the McCartney household where Paul's once outstanding school work had badly slipped. Jim McCartney, however, still hoped that Paul would do well enough to enable him to train as a teacher. Although he had his own plans, Paul, for the time being at least, went along with his father's idea.

At around the same time, Paul began an uneasy friendship with another pupil at the Liverpool Institute. Eighteen months younger than Paul, George Harrison was also a keen guitarist and soon they began to rehearse in George's bedroom.

It was Paul who suggested that The Quarry Men should admit George into their ranks. John, while impressed with George's playing – and the fact that he owned a decent guitar – didn't like the idea of letting a 14-year-old join the band. Undeterred, George became one of the group's most faithful followers, invariably turning up at gigs, guitar in hand. From time to time, if John was feeling generous, he would let him take the odd solo. George, however, had an important ace in his hand – he told John that it would be fine for the band to rehearse at his house at weekends. Thus George Harrison gradually eased himself into The Quarry Men.

THE SILVER BEETLES

Now down to a core of Lennon, McCartney and Harrison, The Quarry Men began playing in various combinations under names such as the Rainbows or

Johnny and the Moondogs.

During this period, John also met another kindred spirit at the art college. Stuart Sutcliffe was a gifted young artist who was destined for great success – everyone from his fellow students to his tutors was agreed on that. Like John, Sutcliffe's appearance also set him apart from the other students. With his skin-tight jeans and brightly coloured shirts, Stu was in no way a Teddy Boy, but he and John quickly became close friends. Stu taught John all about art movements, stoking an interest and enthusiasm that none of his tutors had ever managed. Even though he had never played an instrument or showed any signs of musical ability, John asked him to join the band. Although he had no equipment, the sale of a painting at Liverpool's prestigious Walker Art Gallery earned Sutcliffe enough money to buy a Hofner bass guitar.

Rock 'n' roll peaked in Liverpool in 1960 when Larry Parnes, Britain's great pop impresario, brought US rockers Eddie Cochran and Gene Vincent to play at the Liverpool Empire. The show was a sell-out success and local promoter Alan Williams had the idea of bringing the stars back to the city to play at Liverpool's 6,000-seater boxing arena where they would be supported by Rory Storm and the Hurricanes, far and away the city's most popular rock 'n' roll combo.

Well respected by both John and Paul, The Hurricanes had quickly progressed beyond their skiffle origins and now featured a tight rocking rhythm section. The band's drummer was a mournful-looking young man with rings on every finger. His name was Richard Starkey, but everyone called him Ringo.

The concert was set to be a sell-out when news began to filter through

of a road accident. Eddie Cochran and Gene Vincent had been returning to London from an engagement in Bristol when their car crashed on the A4 near to Chippenham. Vincent had been seriously injured; Cochran was dead. Having already invested huge sums of money in the show, promoter Williams decided that instead of cancelling he would recruit other local bands and make it a showcase for Liverpool's rock 'n' roll talent. The Quarry Men thought this might be their chance and they approached Williams but he was unimpressed. The band which would eventually change the face of pop music was not deemed good enough to even be considered for the bill.

Despite rejecting The Quarry Men, Williams would nonetheless play a part in the group's evolution. He started by giving the band (which had been re-named The Beatals by Sutcliffe as a play on Buddy Holly's backing group, The Crickets) occasional gigs at the Jacaranda coffee bar, which he owned, and was where he based his office, and he also supplied them with their first permanent drummer, 36-year-old Tommy Burns. Unhappy with being tagged The Beatals, the group toyed with the name Long John and the Silver Beetles, but after expressing doubts about being known as Long John, they opted for The Silver Beetles.

Parnes, however, had been deeply impressed with the local talent that Williams put on show. Ever on the look-out for new ways to make or save money, he came up with a brilliantly simple business idea. He began to sign-up singers, rechristen them with memorable names, and tour them round the country accompanied by cheap backing musicians. His biggest new act was former Mersey tug-boat worker Ronald Wycherley, who – as Billy Fury – had become Liverpool's first bona fide rock star, and now needed a backing

band for a national tour. Although The Silver Beetles failed the main audition, Parnes liked them enough to offer them a tour of Scotland backing another new signing named Johnny Gentle.

The tour was supposed to last for just two weeks, but for drummer Burns, it seemed to go on forever. On the second night he was injured when Gentle, worse for wear from the alcohol he invariably used to soothe his stage fright, reversed their van into a parked car. Tommy was in the back of the van, and the entire drum kit fell on top of him. He was rushed off to the local hospital and only managed to limp through the rest of the tour under heavy sedation. When The Silver Beetles returned to Liverpool, he announced his retirement from the music business.

GERMANY CALLING...

As a result of the tour with Gentle, The Silver Beetles were now taken a little more seriously. What's more, Williams had told them that he would find them more engagements when they found a new drummer. At this time Williams was enjoying a new source of business success overseas. He had sent two of his artists to play residencies at the Kaiserkeller club in Hamburg and, according to accounts he was receiving from the club's owner Bruno Koschmider, his band Derry and The Seniors and solo singer Tony Sheridan were both going down a storm. Koschmider was so happy with this new arrangement that he decided to hire a third band to play at another one of his joints – The Indra club. The request posed a problem for Williams,

who wanted to send his top band, Rory Storm and the Hurricanes, but they were already playing a lucrative summer season at Butlins holiday camp in Skegness. Reluctantly, he offered Koschmider The Silver Beetles – or The Beatles, as they now insisted on calling themselves.

The logistics of easing themselves out of their existing responsibilities were not a problem for John and Paul. John was already set to abandon his art school course, while Paul – having just finished his A-level examinations – had effectively left school. George, who had abandoned his schooling at the age of 15, began an apprenticeship as an electrician, but decided to stick with the band. But things were more difficult for Sutcliffe. The talented artist, who everybody said had a great career ahead of him, was about to engage in postgraduate studies at the art college but while clearly the weakest musical link in The Beatles, he agreed to go on the trip after the college reluctantly offered to keep his place open for him.

However, one problem still remained: there was no drummer. The solution came from an unexpected source. the Casbah Club, in the basement of a 14-room house in Haymans Green, had been a popular haunt of bands over

Opposite: Stuart Sutcliffe and Astrid Kirchherr. Stu played bass with The Beatles for two years. He left the group to study art – his principal passion.

Above: Early collaborator Tony Sheridan and The Beatles performing live onstage during The Beatles' first trip to Hamburg, circa 1960.

the years – they had played, rehearsed and hung out there on numerous occasions. The club's owner, Mona Best, had a son who often played drums with the groups that visited. Pete Best was a brilliant pupil and athlete from the Liverpool Collegiate Grammar School, who happened to find himself at a loose end. Like Paul, he had recently completed his A-levels and left school. What's more, his band, The Black Jacks, had just broken up. Without a single rehearsal, Paul offered Best a two-month stint in Hamburg as The Beatles drummer.

The Gentle tour fiasco had been their first real adventure away from home and their families but two months in a foreign land was a different bag altogether. Williams offered to drive The Beatles to Hamburg in his battered old Austin minibus, generously advancing them £15 each so that they could buy a set of matching black crew-neck sweaters from Marks & Spencer. They took few possessions – just their instruments and a small suitcase each – and their only luxury was a tin of home-made scones thoughtfully provided by George's mum.

Planning for the tour had been pretty well non-existent and The Beatles lacked the necessary permits to work legally in Germany. Williams gave them the same advice he offered to all his travelling bands – if questioned at Customs, claim to be visiting students.

On the surface, Hamburg, a port on the north coast of Germany, shared many similarities to Liverpool. The reality, however, came as a shock to the band. Fifteen years after the war had ended, their home city was still full of debris and bomb sites. Hamburg, on the other hand, was feeling the full effect of the German *Wirtschaftswunder* – the great economic recovery. To a bunch of poor working-class kids from Liverpool it was an education – everywhere they looked there seemed to be boutiques and coffee bars.

Sited in the middle of Hamburg's notorious Reeperbahn, an area filled with bright lights, loud music, strip clubs and brothels, the Kaiserkeller Club was a favourite haunt of visiting sailors and just around the corner was The Indra club. Their initial view of Hamburg as the most civilized place on earth vanished the moment they were shown their living quarters. Over the road from The Indra, Koschmider owned a cinema and home for The Beatles for the next two months would be a single room inside that cinema – with the constant drone of German film dialogue audible.

The Beatles' first gigs were a disaster. The band huddled together on a tiny stage and played their set of rock 'n' roll standards before audiences of a dozen or less. Unlike the Kaiserkeller, The Indra had no reputation for live music and

Above: Pete Best in Germany with The Beatles during their first Hamburg season of club dates, circa 1960.

Right: The Indra Club, the first venue in Hamburg The Beatles performed at between August and October 1960.

The Beatles clearly hated it. After continually being goaded by Williams and Koschmider to at least look as if they were enjoying themselves, John took to leaping about manically during the show – no mean feat on such a small stage. As George later remembered: "There was this little guy who used to come around and say 'Mach Schau! Mach Schau!' ['Put on a show!'], so John used to dance around like a gorilla and the rest of us used to knock our heads together."

Little by little, these displays began to attract the interest of clubbers at the raunchier Kaiserkeller. The Beatles quickly turned into a tight rock 'n' roll band. Their workload was heavy: sets often lasted over four hours and they would invariably play more than one set a day. But it was also a fast-track exercise in growing up. They quickly discovered an appetite for the beer that seemed to flow freely plus the women, frequently working prostitutes, who were all too happy to hang out with a bunch of young innocents. The Beatles were also continually tired – they worked hard and getting a good night's sleep at the cinema was impossible. They were introduced to what initially seemed the ideal remedy – Preludin tablets. "Prellies" were slimming tablets that suppressed the appetite and boosted activity. John had a vivid memory of those times: "When the waiters would see the musicians falling over with tiredness or with drink they'd give you the pill ... then you'd be talking, you'd sober up and you could start working almost endlessly until the pill wore off – then you'd take another pill."

Their performances onstage became more and more manic – especially John's whose particular favourite was his impersonation of the crippled rock 'n' roller Gene Vincent. During this first month, The Beatles honed their stage act and grew in confidence. Even though they lived in appalling conditions and had little free time to themselves, John and Paul also began to hone their fledgling songwriting skills, often slipping the results into their live sets.

LEAVING THE INDRA

Escape from the Indra came as a relief to The Beatles. Ever since the club had opened it had been the subject of noise complaints from a neighbour. One day the police finally decided to take action and the club was closed down. Koschmider decided to move The Beatles to the Kaiserkeller. By this time, Williams' biggest earning band, Rory Storm and

Opposite: Tony Sheridan performs on stage with bassist Colin Melander (left) and drummer Ringo Starr at the Top Ten Club in Hamburg, Germany, 1962.

Right: A poster for one of their Hamburg shows with Rory Storm & The Hurricanes (then containing Ringo Starr), October–December 1960.

Far right: The 1957 Gretsch Duo Jet guitar fitted with a Bigsby Vibrato owned by George Harrison and used in the early years with The Beatles.

the Hurricanes, had also arrived for a stint in Hamburg. They had been used to rather better living conditions than those on offer and constantly complained, especially their drummer Richard Starkey, who was known to everybody as "Ringo Starr". During this time, Lou Walters of the Hurricanes booked studio time for some solo recording, with John, Paul and George agreeing to back him. On the day of the session Ringo also came along. The quintet played the popular standards "Fever" and "Summertime" – it was the first time the Fab Four played together.

With a seemingly more serious attitude to life than the others, Sutcliffe had already begun to drift away from the band, spending more and more time with his new artist friends Klaus Voormann and Astrid Kirchherr – a couple who played an active part in the local avant-garde arts scene. When Sutcliffe introduced them to the rest of The Beatles, Kirchherr told them she felt that the band's stage appearance was too haphazard and that they needed a clearer image. She began to make clothes and design a "look" for the group – the first one she came up with was the classic "mop-top" hairstyle. Voormann, meanwhile, began to take artfully posed black-and-white photographs of The Beatles, who were frankly flattered at this kind of attention. Within a short time, Sutcliffe and Kirchherr became inseparable.

Toward the end of the two-month stay, it was clear that The Beatles had become a major attraction at the Kaiserkeller and they were offered another job playing at the much-larger Top Ten Club – a new venue operated by one of Koschmider's bitter rivals. Under veiled threats from their former employer,

the band moved in above the club. There then followed several "coincidental" days of misfortune. First, the police made a routine inspection of the club, demanding to check passports. Discovering George was under 18 and too young to be in a nightclub after midnight, he was immediately packed off to Liverpool. The Beatles tried to carry on at the Top Ten for a few days, with John gamely attempting George's lead guitar solos. The following night, Paul and Pete decided to return to the cinema opposite The Indra to pick up their belongings, but with virtually no lights working in the place, Paul struck a match to see where he was going. He inadvertently started a small fire and, although it caused virtually no damage, Koschmider, still seething over The Beatles' "betrayal", informed the Police. Pete and Paul were traced to the Top Ten Club and arrested. Koschmider agreed to drop the charges but they too were deported. There was nothing left for the others to do, and so Sutcliffe reluctantly took a flight back to England, paid for by Kirchherr, while John jumped on a train wondering what the future held for them back in England.

Below: Stuart Sutcliffe performing live onstage with The Beatles at the Top Ten Club in Hamburg, c. 1960.

Next page/overleaf: Bruno Koschmider's contract with The Beatles, enabling the band to earn their stripes at The Indra club in Hamburg.

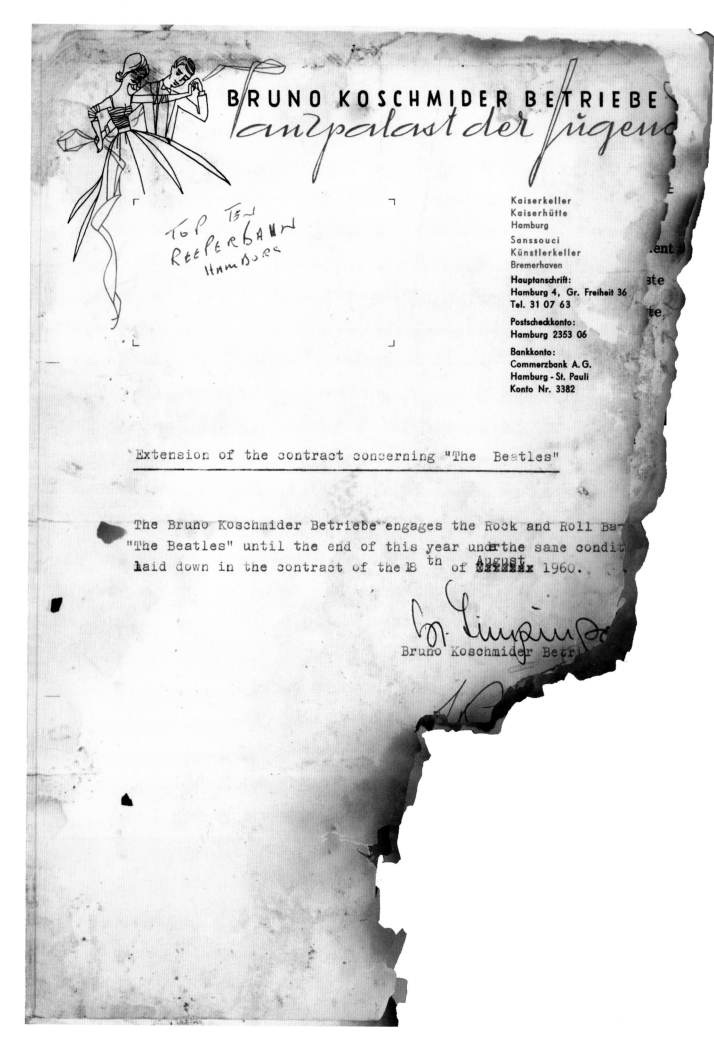

BRUNO KOSCHMIDER BETRIEBE

Tanzpalast der Jugend

Top Ten
Reeperbahn
Hamburg

Kaiserkeller
Kaiserhütte
Hamburg

Sanssouci
Künstlerkeller
Bremerhaven

Hauptanschrift:
Hamburg 4, Gr. Freiheit 36
Tel. 31 07 63

Postscheckkonto:
Hamburg 2353 06

Bankkonto:
Commerzbank A.G.
Hamburg - St. Pauli
Konto Nr. 3382

Extension of the contract concerning "The Beatles"

The Bruno Koschmider Betriebe engages the Rock and Roll Ba[nd]
"The Beatles" until the end of this year und[er] the same condit[ions]
laid down in the contract of the 18 th of August 1960.

Bruno Koschmider Betri[ebe]

ADDITIONAL CLAUSES

1) Should ~~either~~ The Beatles break the contracht they will compensate Mr. Koschmider in full

2) Should Mr. Koschmider break the contract he will be held liable to pay the full fee of engagement for tour.

3) Mr. Koschmider to set working permits for The Beatles.

PLAYING TIMES

esday to Friday playing times 41/2 hours
    pm to 9-30 pm, break 1/2 hour. 10-00 pm to 11-00 pm break 1/2 hour
-30 to 12-30 am break 1/2 hour. 1-00 am to 2 am.

turday playing times 6 hours
00 pm to 8-30 pm break 1/2 hour. 9-00 pm to 10-00 pm break 1/2 hour
-30 pm to 11-30 pm break 1/2 hour. 12-00 to 1-00 am break 1/2 hour
v 0 am to 3-00 am.
h

M day playing times 6 houres
    pm to 6-00 pm break 1/2 hour. 6-30 to 7-30 pm 1/2 hour break.
So to 9-00 pm break 1/2 hour. 9-30 to 10-30 pm break 1/2 hour.
    to 12.00 pm break 1/2 hour. 12-30 to 1-30 am
von
halb
Musi agree to aside to the conditions laid out in
albe e contract.

Opposite: A photograph showing Hamburg's Top Ten Club in 1960.

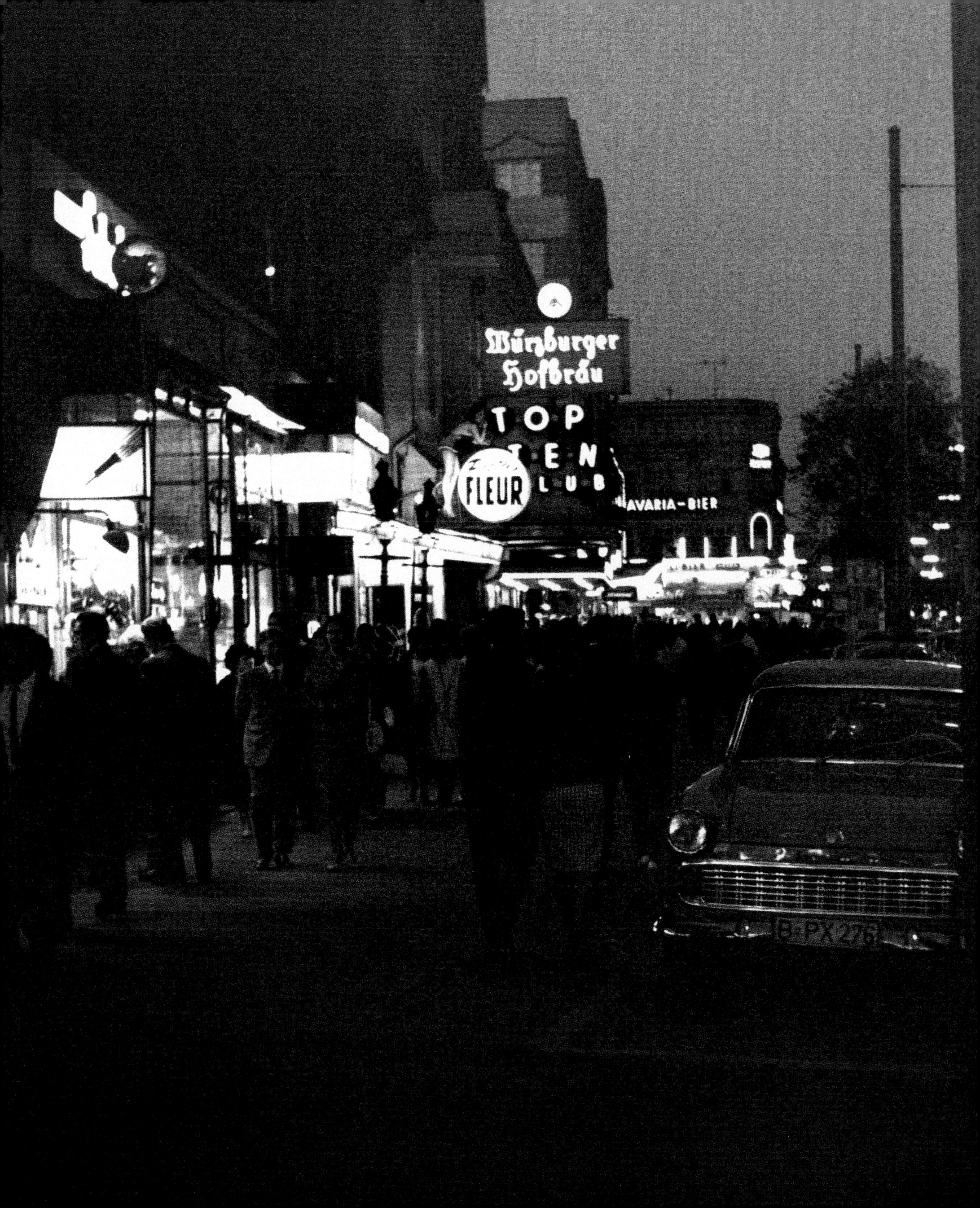

Würzburger
Hofbräu
TOP
TEN
LUB
FLEUR
AVARIA-BIER
B PX 276

1961-1962

THEY

CALLED

IT

"MERSEYBEAT"

THE BEATLES HAD ARRIVED IN GERMANY AS FOUR RELATIVELY INNOCENT YOUNG LADS WITH HOPES OF FUN AND ADVENTURE. THEY RETURNED TO LIVERPOOL DEJECTED, WITH NO CLEAR IDEA OF WHAT TO DO NEXT. IN FACT, THE FIVE OF THEM WERE BACK IN LIVERPOOL FOR ALMOST A MONTH BEFORE THEY EVEN MET UP AGAIN. THEY WERE AMAZED TO FIND A BURGEONING BEAT SCENE DEVELOPING ITS OWN STYLE AND SOUND. TO THEIR GREATER SURPRISE, THE BEATLES DISCOVERED THAT THEIR REPUTATION HAD SPREAD BACK TO LIVERPOOL COURTESY OF THE OTHER MERSEY BANDS RETURNING FROM STINTS IN HAMBURG.

Their first gig back in their home town was at the Casbah Club, owned by Pete Best's mother. Instead of the apathy they had previously encountered, their powerful new sound and confident performance transfixed the audience. The Beatles had left Liverpool as a bunch of enthusiastic no-hopers and returned as one of the City's hottest acts.

Liverpool seemed to be changing by the day. Ray McFall, owner of The Cavern jazz club, had noticed the popularity of the new beat groups, and had started to introduce them at lunchtime sessions in his club. At the end of January 1961, the new-look Beatles started playing at The Cavern. They were offered a block booking for which they were paid 25 shillings (£1.25) per day. For this they would have to play two 45-minute stints each day – hardly demanding for a band more used to five-hour, amphetamine-fuelled sets in Hamburg's clubs.

The Beatles in concert were now positively electric, and quickly becoming a huge local attraction. It was now that they first began to experience the screaming teenage girls who would soon come to dominate their lives, and provide a poignant snapshot of a whole era. And the object of much of this early adulation was the band's handsome drummer, Best. Yet in spite of their growing popularity, there were the first signs of disharmony in The Beatles camp. Stuart Sutcliffe was all too aware that he was the weakest link in the band, while Paul – tiring of Sutcliffe's musical limitations – was vocal in his desire to take on the role of bass guitarist. It was only John Lennon's sturdy defence of his art-school friend that kept him in the group.

EXIT STU

In April 1961, The Beatles were offered the chance to return to Hamburg, this time, playing at the Top Ten Club where they would each earn £40 per week (twice as much as before). This was considerably more than any of them could have earned doing unskilled work back home in Liverpool. In Germany, they would alternate sets throughout the night with singer Tony Sheridan.

Sutcliffe was thrilled to be back with Astrid Kirschherr, but he was becoming less and less enthusiastic about The Beatles and it was his girlfriend who encouraged him to enroll as a student at the Hamburg State Art College. This was a particularly attractive prospect as Eduardo Paolozzi, one of Sutcliffe's idols, had been appointed to run a series of master classes there. Paolozzi was highly impressed by the work he was shown, and not only admitted Sutcliffe to the course but also managed to get him a state bursary. From that point, Sutcliffe gradually stepped back from the band. He never formally left The Beatles – Paul just gradually played the bass more and more often until Stuart stopped turning up.

During this second Hamburg visit The Beatles cut their first record. Discovering both Tony Sheridan and The Beatles playing at the Top Ten, producer Bert Kaempfert invited them to his studio to record a single. The songs he chose were seemingly unlikely candidates – folk song "My Bonnie Lies Over The Ocean" and New Orleans jazz standard "When the Saints Go Marching In" – but they were given the rock 'n' roll treatment. Renamed the Beat Brothers for the project, the single hit the German Top 10 and turned Sheridan into a minor star. The Beatles made little money from this venture – they had each received a one-off payment of 300 marks (about £25) – but the recording studio experience was an invaluable one.

"RIGHT THEN, BRIAN, MANAGE US."

Returning to Liverpool, it seemed that the beat revolution was now everywhere. There was even a Liverpool music paper, *Mersey Beat*. Started by

Previous spread: The Beatles during their first professional photography session with local wedding photographer Albert Marrion near Liverpool, December 17, 1961.

Opposite: Hamburg's Star-Club opened in 1962 and would host many of the greats of rock music throughout the 1960s.

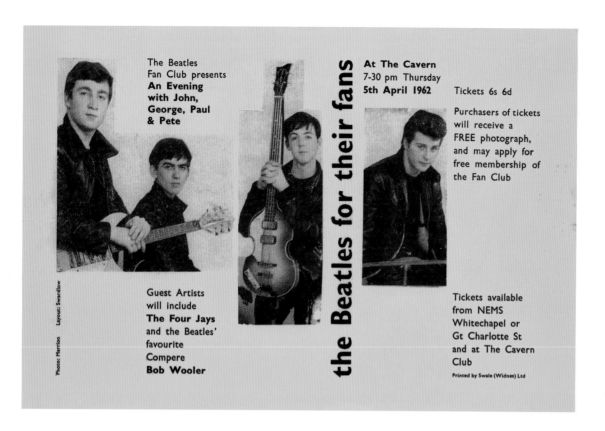

The Beatles
Fan Club presents
**An Evening
with John,
George, Paul
& Pete**

the Beatles for their fans

At The Cavern
7-30 pm Thursday
5th April 1962

Tickets 6s 6d

Purchasers of tickets
will receive a
FREE photograph,
and may apply for
free membership of
the Fan Club

Guest Artists
will include
The Four Jays
and the Beatles'
favourite
Compere
Bob Wooler

Tickets available
from NEMS
Whitechapel or
Gt Charlotte St
and at The Cavern
Club

Printed by Swale (Widnes) Ltd

Left: A 1962 flyer for The (Pete Best era) Beatles, playing at the legendary Cavern Club in Liverpool, April 5, 1962.

Opposite: An early photograph of the Fab Four.

Bill Harry, a young art student and music enthusiast, it would play a significant role in The Beatles' early successes. Harry had known John from art school and remembered his fondness for drawing witty and scurrilous cartoons. For the first issue of *Mersey Beat* he asked John to write an amusing story on how The Beatles started. "A Short Diversion on the Dubious Origins of The Beatles" and other similarly surreal articles that John contributed to the magazine helped to separate The Beatles from the fierce competition that they now faced from other local groups.

One of *Mersey Beat*'s first local business customers had been the NEMS electrical shop – "The Finest Record Selection in the North", as its adverts proudly proclaimed. The shop was one of a chain run by the Epsteins, a wealthy and prominent Jewish family. Dapper in appearance, always dressed in a well-cut tailor-made suit, 27-year-old Brian Epstein took great pride in being able to obtain any record his customers might have wanted. During one week a succession of teenagers came in asking for The Beatles' recording of "My Bonnie". But no matter how many record company availability lists he scanned, Epstein could find no mention of its existence. Discovering that they were, in fact, a local band who were currently playing at The Cavern, Epstein felt compelled to find out more about this mysterious group. Catching one of The Beatles' lunchtime sets, he was quite taken aback by what he saw: "This was quite a new world really for me. I was amazed by this dank atmosphere ... they were somewhat ill-clad and the presentation left a little to be desired. Amongst this, however, something tremendous came over. I was really just struck by their music, the beat and their sense of humour on stage. Even afterwards, when I met them, I was struck again by their personal charm. It was there it all started."

In the early 1960s, homosexuality was far from commonly accepted and in a tough, industrial city like Liverpool it could be a life-threatening admission. Epstein had been a practising homosexual for many years, living a secret double life that contrasted his "respectable" public image with a twilight world that sought out like-minded souls. It might have been that the sight of four young men in tight black leather clothes sweating away onstage was one that excited him. But seeing the effect The Beatles were having on the lunchtime crowds – of both sexes – certainly appealed to his business instincts. Epstein made several further visits. The Beatles began to notice this curious-looking man in their audience with a suit and briefcase and eventually, in November 1961, Epstein arranged to meet the band after one of their Cavern performances. He offered them his services as a manager. After Paul had satisfied himself that Brian would play no role in their music, they all agreed.

By the end of 1961, as far as the Mersey bands were concerned, The Beatles were now top of the pile. Yet outside the area, even in Manchester, they were largely unknown. Epstein was certain that the only way of breaking The Beatles was to bring them to the attention of the major London-based record companies. Getting his band an audition would not be difficult: as the manager of one of the biggest record stores in the north of England, no label would want to risk upsetting him unnecessarily. As far as Epstein was concerned, all he had to do was get the labels to listen to his band: their music would do the talking.

The first label Epstein courted was Decca – one of the most powerful of Britain's record companies. The audition would take place at their London studio at 165 Broadhurst Gardens, in West Hampstead on the first day of January, 1962. The recording process was crude by today's standards. There was no overdubbing, The Beatles simply plugged in their instruments, the engineer set recording levels, and the band played. In the space of a few hours 15 tracks had been laid down.

The Beatles were by no means happy with their performance, but everyone thought it would be enough to a secure a deal. Decca boss Dick Rowe, however, declined to sign The Beatles. In one of pop music's most celebrated errors of judgement, Rowe informed Brian Epstein that he didn't want the band because "groups with guitars are on the way out". A few years later John and Paul would remember this incident – Paul: "He must be kicking himself now", John: "I hope he kicks himself to death."

THE NEW LOOK

Disappointed with Decca's rebuttal, Epstein turned his attention to the band's public image. First, he tried to instill a sense of discipline. The Beatles may have been *Mersey Beat*'s top band, but they also had a reputation for unreliability which worried serious promoters. Epstein produced a series of typed memoranda for each member of the band detailing the new regime. Punctuality was in, shouting at mates in the audience was out, working to an agreed set list with no deviations was in, belching into the microphone – a great favourite with John – was also out.

Most important, though, the black leather outfits that they had taken to wearing, under the influence of Sutcliffe and Kirchherr in Hamburg, had to go. Black leather, Epstein reasoned, had too many connotations with troublemakers. He took them to a local bespoke tailor and had them measured up for a set of matching brushed-tweed grey lounge suits with narrow velvet collars. John still managed to have his say: "My little rebellion was to have my tie loose with the top button of my shirt undone, but McCartney would always come up to me and put it straight." Paul was already beginning to be seen as the ambitious one – if they had to wear these dreadful suits to make it, then that was fine by him. After all, they hadn't

exactly set the world alight doing their own thing.

In March of 1962, Epstein booked The Beatles to open a major new venue in Hamburg – the Star-Club. The band were clearly moving up in the world now and instead of being huddled in the back of an old van driving through England and Holland to the North of Germany, they took a flight from Manchester's Ringway airport. They were looking forward to seeing their old mates, not least Sutcliffe and Kirchherr. In spite of having been edged out of the band, Sutcliffe and John had remained close friends, writing to each other frequently. But they arrived in Hamburg to hear some terrible news. Sutcliffe was dead. He had recently suffered a spate of increasingly serious headaches and the cause of death cited on his death certificate was "cerebral paralysis due to bleeding into the right ventricle of the brain". The band was devastated – Pete and George cried continually. Only John, trying his hardest to keep his tough Scouse persona intact, refused to crack, but everybody close to the band knew that he was the one who had been hardest hit.

While The Beatles were doing their thing in Hamburg, Epstein was busy in London trying to get them a deal. He had now tried hawking their Decca demo to every reasonably sized label he could find. Having hit on the idea of having a demonstration disc to play to prospective labels, he went to the HMV store in London's Oxford Street. Here it was possible to have one-off records cut from a master tape. Epstein's arrival at the HMV shop began a sequence of good fortune. It started when the engineer who processed the record took an

immediate liking to the sound of the band. He suggested that Epstein take it to Sid Coleman, EMI's head of publishing, who was located in the same building. Coleman also liked what he heard and immediately agreed to publish two of the songs – the Lennon and McCartney compositions "Love of the Loved" and "Hello Little Girl". This was a major breakthrough. Epstein expressed his gratitude but patiently explained that while he would be more than happy to sign a publishing deal – with EMI's Ardmore & Beechwood division – he was really after a recording contract for The Beatles. Coleman picked up the phone and called his friend George Martin, at that time head of A&R for Parlophone, one of the smaller subsidiaries of the vast EMI empire.

George Martin was unusual among A&R men in the pop field. There was little trace of the "Tin Pan Alley" mentality in his approach to finding new artists and material. Martin had received a classical grounding, having studied piano and oboe at London's Guildhall School of Music. On graduating, he had joined the BBC's music library, but soon grew bored and took a job at EMI. By the age of 30 he was running EMI's Parlophone label, one that had enjoyed most of its successes with comedy or novelty recordings. Martin had reluctantly begun looking for talent among the countless newly formed electric beat groups. So it was with no great expectations that Martin listened politely to the demonstration record brought to him by this smartly dressed, softly spoken

Liverpool man. Martin was impressed by George's guitar work and Paul's vocals, but he heard little on offer that distinguished The Beatles from many other competent beat groups. And yet, as he later said, "I thought to myself: 'There might *just* be something there.'" He offered to record the band.

EMI's Abbey Road Studios were situated in a large detached house in the middle of St John's Wood, a well-appointed area of north London. The recording would take place on June 6, 1962 in Studio 3, the smallest suite in the complex. Again, The Beatles concentrated on their usual mix of standards and their own material. After Epstein had sent them a telegram in Hamburg telling them about the EMI session, John and Paul immediately began work on new material. The songs that emerged were far stronger than their previous efforts, showing a new level of confidence. The two surviving songs from this session

Below: With American rock and roll musician Gene Vincent (1935–1971) at the Star Club, Hamburg, April–May 1962.

Opposite: John Lennon live on stage at the Cavern Club in Matthew Street, Liverpool, December 1961.

Next spread: Another shot from The Beatles' first professional photoshoot, Liverpool, December 1961.

Left: A flyer for the farewell performance of "The Beetles" at Tower Ballroom, Brighton, prior to a two-month season in Germany.

Opposite: Ex-Beatles drummer Pete Best, far right, and his new group the Pete Best Four.

are The Coasters' hit "Besame Mucho" sung with great charm by Paul. The other was a new composition, "Love Me Do", written by John and Paul.

PROBLEMS WITH THE DRUMMER

Martin liked he heard, but just didn't find it exciting enough. The standards, he thought, were all too corny, but he also feared that the self-penned material was not commercial enough. He was, however, certain that Best was not a good enough drummer to use on recordings. He told Epstein that if The Beatles made a record for Parlophone he would insist on using Andy White, his own session drummer. Martin mulled over the matter for a further month before offering The Beatles a one-year contract, the bare minimum to which the label would commit.

Then the issue of what to do about Best became Epstein's immediate problem. When the other members found out the producer's views, Paul

and George were keen to sack him just to get the matter out of the way. The Cavern gig on Wednesday August 15 turned out to be Best's last as a drummer with The Beatles. The following day, he was called to Epstein's office and told the news: "Pete, the boys want you out of the group. They don't think you're a good enough drummer."

It would be the end of Best's music career. Being ejected from the band was bad enough, but unable to hide from their headline-capturing successes over the coming years would prove to be a severely testing time for the hurt and angry drummer. Best could be seen as simply the unluckiest man in the history of pop music – the clearest possible example of how little consolation there is in the word "nearly".

There was now turbulence in The Beatles' camp. Throughout the sacking of Best, one voice had been uncharacteristically quiet – John had other things on his mind. To his complete horror, Cynthia Powell, his long-standing girlfriend from art school, told him that she was pregnant. Unexpectedly, perhaps, Lennon the rebel – using the vernacular of the day – chose to "do the decent thing." The day after Best was fired from the band, John and Cynthia were married at Liverpool's Mount Pleasant Registry Office.

Filling The Beatles' drum stool was now the most urgent priority. At the top of their recruitment list was Ringo Starr, Rory Storm's drummer. By the summer of 1962, Ringo had begun to lose enthusiasm for a career in music, but had agreed to do one final holiday camp season with Storm. It was John who convinced the drummer to rethink his retirement plans. Phoning him at the Butlins holiday camp in Skegness, on England's east coast, John invited him to join The Beatles.

Meanwhile, an unexpected crisis was brewing in Liverpool. *Mersey Beat* had broken the news of Best's sacking, resulting in an outcry from his many female fans. They mounted all-night vigils outside his house, and even began to picket The Cavern. A week after Best's departure, the cameras of regional TV show *Know the North* visited The Cavern to film The Beatles: the closing chords of "Some Other Guy" are clearly punctuated not only by the usual cheering and screaming, but voices crying out "We want Pete!"

Epstein was thoroughly bemused by all the fuss. It was common knowledge among his close gay friends that it had not been the pretty-boy Best, nor the fresh-faced looks of George or Paul that had attracted him to the band, but John Lennon – the guy who sometimes called him the "Queer Jew" – whose sharp tongue and acid humour would prove a gift and a curse later in his career in that they could charm an audience but also court controversy…

"YOUR FIRST NO. 1"

The sessions to produce the first Beatles' single were to take place on September 6 and 11, 1962. Producer George Martin had decided that the best approach from the start would be to use original compositions. He selected two tracks "P.S. I Love You" and "Love Me Do" but he had not been told about The Beatles' new drummer and had already hired Andy White for the session. The recordings took place at Abbey Road Studio Two, a sophisticated environment that enabled The Beatles to lay down a backing track with no vocals or lead parts played – these would be overdubbed afterwards. Ringo was allowed to take part in the second session. Martin was pleasantly surprised by what he heard, but still didn't consider Ringo to be up to the standard of his own drummer. The sessions yielded two versions of "Love Me Do", with White playing on one and Ringo on the other. Three weeks later, on October 4, 1962, the version with White on drums was released as The Beatles' first single. George Martin later joked: "Ringo to this day bears those scars. He'll say to me 'You didn't let me play, did you?'" But Ringo recalled the distress he felt: "It was devastating … he [Andy White] wasn't doing anything so great that I couldn't do it."

Outside Liverpool, The Beatles were still an unknown quantity. During the first week after the record's release nothing much seemed to happen. It was given an airing on Radio Luxembourg, but that was about all. Epstein, knowing the numbers required to get a record into the charts, realized there was only one thing for it – through NEMS he bought 10,000 copies of the singles from Parlophone. While the record caused a

Right: Two posters advertising concerts at the Tower Ballroom in Merseyside, UK, 1961.

Opposite: Girls dancing at the Cavern Club, where The Beatles staged their first performance in 1961.

Opposite: George Harrison on stage at Star-Club in Hamburg, May 1962.

Right: The Beatles performing prior to signing their first recording contract, Liverpool, 1962.

Below: A flyer for The Beatles at a lunchtime rock session at the Liverpool Jazz Society.

sensation in Liverpool and went straight to the top of the *Mersey Beat* charts, the vast majority of Epstein's stock gathered dust in the NEMS storeroom. Finally, the single made a showing in the national *New Musical Express* chart at No. 27. By the middle of December it peaked at No. 17.

It was a small beginning, but it did bring The Beatles to a national audience for the first time, and Martin offered the band a five-year contract. The Beatles were back in the studio at the end of November to record a second single. Both Epstein and Martin favoured a song brought to them by music publisher Dick James. "How Do You Do It?" was a new composition by Mitch Murray, one of James' in-house composers. Everyone who heard the number was convinced that it would top the charts, irrespective of who recorded it. The Beatles, however, had their own ideas. They wanted to persevere with their own material, especially a gutsy new number, "Please Please Me", which showed off the band's vocal harmony skills to the full. During the recording, Martin instinctively knew that it was going to be a massive hit. At the end of the session he pressed the studio intercom button to speak to the band: "Gentlemen," he announced, "you have just made your first No. 1."

Although The Beatles had turned down "How Do You Do It?" another of Epstein's growing roster of Liverpool artists, Gerry and the Pacemakers, would take the song to the top of the charts in March, 1963. James was sufficiently impressed with The Beatles to suggest the formation of Northern Songs, a company set up with Epstein to exclusively administer Lennon and McCartney compositions. James was able to use his influence immediately, arranging a TV appearance for The Beatles to perform "Please Please Me" on the Saturday night pop show *Thank Your Lucky Stars*. Further exposure would follow on the pop show that reviewed new releases, *Juke Box Jury*. Both would coincide with the release of the new single in January 1963.

'Swinging Lunch Time Rock Sessions'
AT THE
LIVERPOOL JAZZ SOCIETY,
13, TEMPLE STREET (off Dale Street and Victoria Street),
EVERY LUNCH TIME, 12-00 to 2-30
RESIDENT BANDS:
Gerry and the Pacemakers,
Rory Storm and the Wild Ones,
The Big Three.

Next Wednesday Afternoon, March 15th
12-00 to 5-00 Special
STARRING—
The Beatles,
Gerry and the Pacemakers
Rory Storm and the Wild Ones.
Admission—Members 1/-, Visitors 1/6
" Rocking at the L. J. S. "

The Victor Printing Co. 230, West Derby Road, Liverpool, 6

After years of struggling, The Beatles suddenly seemed to have made enormous progress in the space of a few months. It was all too easy to forget that they still had a contractual obligation that dated back to the summer for a two-week engagement at the Star-Club in Hamburg but this no longer held any great appeal. The band had already hit the UK Top 20 and saw the gig as time wasted, potentially keeping them out of the British public eye. To make matters worse they were not even top of the bill, but were supporting Johnny and the Hurricanes, an American instrumental band, who, by 1962, were a couple of years past their biggest hits like "Red River Rock" and "Beatnik Fly". In the event, The Beatles acquitted themselves with barely adequate aplomb. Their playing was, by their own admission, less than perfect – a fact clearly audible on the recordings that were released, against the wishes of the band, 15 years later.

1962 may have been an extraordinary year – they'd earned a record deal with EMI, had their first hit single and the readers of music magazine *New Musical Express* had voted them fifth best British vocal group – but right now they were stuck in Hamburg. They were bored. They were tired. It was Christmas and they were away from their families and friends. They couldn't wait to get away from the place.

Above: The Beatles performing on stage at the Star-Club, Hamburg, April–May 1962.

Opposite: Hamburg's Star-Club opened in 1962 and would host many of the greats of rock music throughout the 1960s.

1 9 6 3

BEATLEMANIA

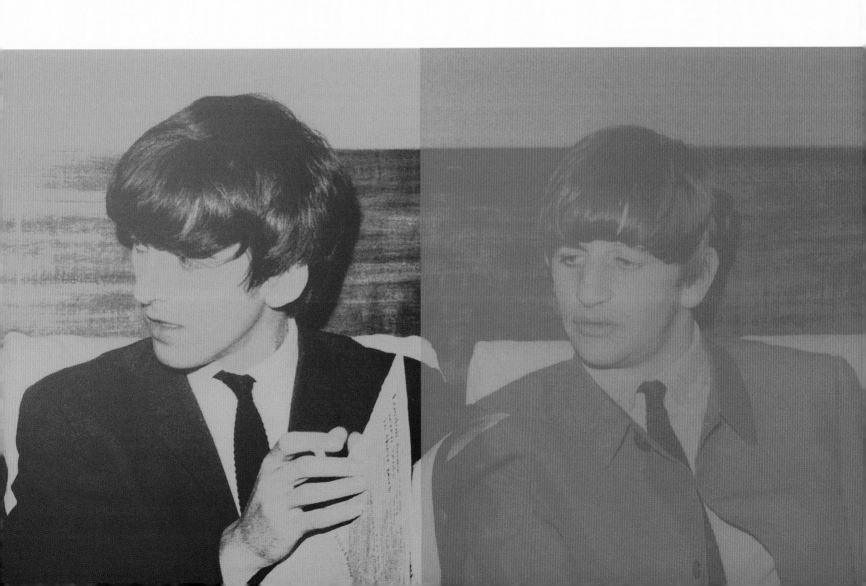

THE BEATLES FLEW BACK TO THE UK ON THE SECOND DAY OF 1963. BUT THERE WAS NO TIME FOR REST – A BRIEF FIVE-DAY EXCURSION NORTH OF THE BORDER IN SCOTLAND HAD ALREADY BEEN ARRANGED, STARTING THE FOLLOWING DAY. HOWEVER, EXCITEMENT WAS IN THE AIR AS THE NEW SINGLE, "PLEASE PLEASE ME", WAS DUE FOR RELEASE ANY DAY AND EVERYONE HAD HIGH HOPES FOR A BIG SUCCESS. AFTER ALL, GEORGE MARTIN, THEIR PRODUCER, HAD MORE OR LESS GUARANTEED IT.

Despite their optimism, the tour started on a disastrous note. That winter had been one of the worst in living memory and, as always, Scotland had been much more seriously affected than the rest of the UK. The first gig on the tour was in the town of Keith - one of the stops on their ill-fated Johnny Gentle tour two years earlier. However, the weather worsened during the day and snowdrifts made many of the Highland roads impassable. Their plane was forced to land at Aberdeen instead of Edinburgh, but when they arrived they were told that the show had been cancelled. The four remaining dates went ahead successfully, if uneventfully; The Beatles were biding their time.

January 11 was the big day. "Please, Please Me" hit record shops throughout the nation. Epstein and publisher James put a combined effort into publicizing the new release, starting with the slot on *Thank Your Lucky Stars*. Although made by the Birmingham-based ABC television company, the programme was broadcast throughout Great Britain's independent television networks. On Sunday January 12, The Beatles turned up to the ATV studios in Aston, near Birmingham to mime their new single in front of a wild teenage audience. The following Wednesday they delivered a similarly mimed performance for Granada TV's *People and Places* programme. The next day they were booked for two live performances on their home territory – a Cavern session at lunchtime, and then down the road to Birkenhead's Majestic Ballroom later that evening. The Majestic gig had sold out well in advance, leaving 500 disappointed fans trying to get in on the night.

The frenzied promotion continued apace. Positive reviews of "Please Please Me" began to emerge. *New Musical Express* praised it as "full of vigour and vitality", while BBC radio's Brian Matthew – an influential figure in his day – rated them as the best thing he'd heard since The Shadows. However, none of this could compete with the impact of television and, even thought they were effectively bottom of the bill, The Beatles created a sensation when *Thank Your Lucky Stars* was aired on January 19.

The band, with their "mop-top" fringes and buttoned up suits, presented an image that clearly set them apart from other groups. Above all, The Beatles refused to appear mean and moody like so many other rock 'n' rollers; instead, they bounced around the television screen with beaming grins. This didn't look like a choreographed act, it looked as if they were four lads having a good time. And it was very infectious.

Their music was also different. The driving energy and use of high-pitched falsetto vocals created a unique effect. It was a technique that they had taken from the dramatic – almost operatic – singles that Roy Orbison had recorded a few years earlier. "Please Please Me" was the first public outing for what would soon become one of the hallmarks of the early Beatles sound. It was clear from their TV performance that shifting the dynamic in this way had a clear impact on their teenage audience – it made them scream more loudly!

HITTING THE TOP

At the beginning of February, with "Please Please Me" about to make its entry into the Top 10, The Beatles embarked on their first-ever national tour, opening a six-act bill that starred the singer Helen Shapiro. In 1961, as a 14-year-old schoolgirl, Shapiro had burst onto the British pop scene with "Walking Back to Happiness", but barely two years later her career was already on the wane. This tour, it was hoped, would establish her as one of Britain's top female vocalists.

On February 10, The Beatles travelled down to London for another recording session with George Martin. Satisfied with their growing success, Martin still thought they were capable of a good deal better. The purpose of the session was to record a debut album that captured the energy of their live set – something many performers have tried to achieve but rarely with success. However, one thing the recordings certainly captured was spontaneity. The Beatles started work in Studio 2 of Abbey Road at ten in the morning and carried on until eleven o'clock at night, stopping only briefly for lunch and dinner. The recordings were produced by Martin with his engineer Norman "Hurricane" Smith. In the space of barely 13 hours they recorded a staggering 79 takes of 14 songs. Eight of them were Lennon-McCartney originals and the other six were covers from their stage show. Over the following month Martin would decide which takes they would use on the album.

Nowadays it would be hard to imagine a major recording artist producing an LP in a single day – indeed, it's more common for albums to be drawn out over a period of several years. For The Beatles, the process was a simple one: they plugged in and played. It was all largely recorded live, with a bare minimum of vocal and instrumental overdubs. And the next day they went straight back to work, performing in different venues throughout the country pretty much every day of the week.

On March 2, 1963, Martin's prediction was fulfilled. After hovering in the Top 10 for a few weeks, "Please Please Me" went to the top of the charts. Once again, timing proved to be problematic for The Beatles. A month or so earlier, they had taken part in a short tour supporting a pair of American singers, Tommy Roe and Chris Montez. It quickly became evident from the reaction of the audience that it was The Beatles who were the main draw.

While on the second leg of the Helen Shapiro tour, John and Paul had written a new song – "Misery" – which they had hoped she would record but ended up being covered by Kenny Lynch. At this time, of course, the notion of a "career pop star" was seen as an absurd idea, since many within the industry thought that rock 'n' roll and beat music was just a passing fad. John himself didn't necessarily expect The Beatles to enjoy a lengthy time in the limelight: he imagined that he and Paul would ultimately pursue a professional songwriting partnership. Ironically, since they had signed the

Previous spread: The Fab Four take a coffee break from rehearsals for the Royal Variety Performance, November 4, 1963.

Above: The Beatles in 1963: Paul McCartney, George Harrison, Ringo Starr and John Lennon.

MEMORIAL HALL
NORTHWICH

LEWIS BUCKLEY ENTERTAINMENTS, LTD.
PRESENT

SAT. APRIL 27   7/6 Pay at door

HIT RECORDERS OF "PLEASE, PLEASE ME"

THE
BEATLES
DENNY CURTIS AND THE RENEGADES
THE CRUISERS WITH KARL TERRY

★ ★ ★ ★ ★ ★ ★

SAT. MAY 4   6/6 Pay at door

RECORDERS OF "SOUNDS LIKE LOCOMOTION" FROM "SATURDAY CLUB"
"THANK YOUR LUCKY STARS" AND "EASY BEAT"—THE DYNAMIC

SOUNDS
INCORPORATED
THE FOUR JUST MEN
BRUCE HARRIS AND THE CAVALIERS

DANCING 7.45—11.45 P.M.
USUAL LATE TRANSPORT

ARTHURS, WOODCHESTER, STROUD

Opposite: A poster for The Beatles' performance at Memorial Hall, Northwich, April 27, 1963.

Right: A flyer for The Beatles at the Odeon Theatre, Luton, September 6, 1963.

publishing contract that created Northern Songs, Lennon and McCartney were increasingly writing on their own – even if often helping each other out with ideas. Nonetheless, throughout the lifetime of The Beatles their songs were always registered as joint compositions.

At a recording session on March 5, The Beatles performed 13 takes of both "From Me To You" and an older composition, "Thank You Little Girl". As a footnote to this session, with some remaining studio time they quickly rushed through a couple of takes of "The One After 909" and "What Goes On". Neither of these songs saw the light of day at the time, but new versions reappeared on later albums.

With "Please Please Me" a smash hit, The Beatles were becoming big news. The national press, which rarely reported on teenage interests, began to travel to Liverpool to interview the band. One such interviewer was Maureen Cleave of London's *Evening Standard*, the first journalist to give the group a wider, more considered coverage. In her interview she was struck by the mischievous and sharp wit of these four bright young lads and John in particular. She could see how infectious their enthusiasm was. Cleave was, perhaps, the first journalist to capture the essence of The Beatles interacting as mates, something that became such a staple for their debut film, *A Hard Day's Night* (1964). It was now six years since John had dreamed of making The Quarry Men a success. Now, at least, people were sitting up and taking notice – even if the majority of them still saw The Beatles as an overnight success.

As the band's first No. 1 began its inevitable fall from the top of the charts, Parlophone released The Beatles' debut album on March 22. To cash in on the success of the single, it was entitled *Please Please Me*. After all, Martin still wasn't convinced that they would avoid the pitfalls of so many one- or two-hit wonders. He need not have worried – the album came straight into the LP charts at No. 9.

THE MERSEY INVASION

The national success of The Beatles created an unexpected knock-on effect. The British music industry, based largely in London, quickly learned that there had been a serious music scene going on in the North of England, which they knew very little about. Epstein, more than anyone else, helped to put what was now being called "Merseybeat" on the map. By the middle of 1963, Epstein's NEMS Enterprises had a roster that in retrospect reads like an A-Z of early 60s British pop. He signed up the best that Liverpool could produce and, setting up new head office in London, used the success of The Beatles to get his new acts recording contracts. More often than not, Epstein's bands found fame with compositions written by John and Paul.

Liverpool's other big success story of the time was Gerry and the Pacemakers. They created a record that even The Beatles were unable to match, by their first three singles going to the top of the charts. Indeed, the Pacemakers began this run of hits with "How Do You Do It?", the song The Beatles had turned down.

Among the other Liverpool bands to experience a taste of success were Billy J. Kramer and the Dakotas and The Fourmost, both of whom enjoyed a number of Lennon and McCartney hits. The Searchers also enjoyed a lengthy career, mostly playing covers of unknown American hits – such as "Sugar and Spice", "Sweets For My Sweet" and "Needles and Pins" – which all managed high chart placings.

However, there were others in Liverpool who struggled to come to grips with these changes in the group's fortune – The Beatles' families. John's Aunt Mimi – who now also provided a home for his wife Cynthia and their baby son Julian – was completely bewildered as teenage girls kept a continuous vigil outside the house, hoping for an increasingly rare appearance of the Beatle. It was the same for the other families. Elsie Gleave, Ringo's mother, couldn't believe how much money her son now seemed to have. In fact, she wasn't convinced that Ringo's business was entirely legal.

UK label:
Parlophone PMC 1202/
PCS 3042

Release Date:
April 1963

US label:
EMI US C2-46435-2

Release Date:
February 1987

Producer:
George Martin

SIDE 1

I Saw Her Standing There (Lennon/McCartney)
Misery (Lennon/McCartney)
Anna (Go To Him) (Alexander)
Chains (Goffin/King)
Boys (Dixon/Farrell)
Ask Me Why (Lennon/McCartney)
Please Please Me (Lennon/McCartney)

SIDE 2

Love Me Do (Lennon/McCartney)
P.S. I Love You (Lennon/McCartney)
Baby It's You (David/Williams/Bacharach)
Do You Want To Know A Secret (Lennon/McCartney)
A Taste Of Honey (Scott/Marlow)
There's A Place (Lennon/McCartney)
Twist And Shout (Medley/Russell)

The Beatles themselves also had to adjust to the way they were now treated. For Ringo this even extended to his family: "I was at my auntie's and we were having a cup of tea one night ... someone knocked into the coffee table and some of my tea spilled into the saucer. Suddenly it was 'He can't have that now' and they took it away and gave me a clean saucer. That would never have happened before! I thought, hmm, things are changing!"

On April 11, Parlophone released the third Beatles single, "From Me To You". A little slower than its predecessor, its ingredients were much the same but music critics were not overly impressed. To The Beatles, though, it was a good progression. As Paul said, "We were always just trying to improve on what we and other people we heard were doing...It was nice when we got that minor chord in the middle of 'From Me To You'. It was something we hadn't done before."

Sunday, April 21 saw The Beatles playing their biggest gig to date, to a crowd of 10,000 people at the *New Musical Express* poll winners show, held in the Empire Pool, Wembley. The major attraction was Cliff Richard and The Shadows, but The Beatles were now second on the bill. A week later "From Me To You" went straight to the top of the charts, sold over a half-a-million copies and scored the band their first silver disc.

After a frenzied year, The Beatles needed a break. As John would later say of the period, "We had to do an album in 12 hours and a new single every three months. We'd be writing new songs literally in the hotel or in the van." Epstein decided that they should all have two weeks off. Paul, George and Ringo took their girlfriends off to Tenerife for 11 days. Meanwhile, Brian and John flew off to Spain, leaving Cynthia and Julian with Aunt Mimi. Over the years, John's holiday with Epstein has prompted all kinds of speculation as to the true nature of their relationship, including a fictionalized television drama. Needless to say there was never any response from either party.

MORE OF THE SAME

Refreshed after their break, The Beatles came back to an unexpected surprise; in their absence the album had gone to the top of the charts, and looked destined to be one of the year's top sellers. What's more, they were about to embark on a third national tour, this time with Roy Orbison – one of their great heroes. The Beatles and Gerry and the Pacemakers were to be second and third on the bill. Inevitably, however, audience reaction betrayed the real stars of the

show. Quickly, and with a sense of unease given the awe with which they held Roy Orbison, The Beatles became top of the bill.

Radio shows, TV appearances and all kinds of offers arrived day after day, yet The Beatles were still performing live five times a week. After a show in Newcastle on June 26, John and Paul got together in their hotel room to see if they could write their next single. They were now beginning to feel the pressure; there had been two No. 1 hits in succession, and anything less would be a disaster for the band. As they talked and fiddled with their acoustic guitars, John made a suggestion that instead of writing about "me and you" they try something about a third person. Paul, again stressing the band's desire to keep moving forward, remembers, "We hit on the idea of doing a reported conversation – 'She told me what to say, she said she loves you' – giving it a dimension that was different to what we'd done before."

The song they came up with was "She Loves You". Five days later they went back to Abbey Road to record it. An instant classic, everyone who heard the finished track knew that the band had produced something special. Combining the characteristics that had already made The Beatles so popular, it also featured the irresistible "yeah, yeah, yeah" chorus – one of the most famous hooklines in the history of pop music.

The single was released on Friday, August 23, 1963, with a gentle ballad, "I'll Get You", featured on the flip side. "She Loves You" went straight to the No. 1 spot, selling half-a-million copies within the first two weeks. It also had an unusually long chart life for a single, staying at the top for a month, dropping back into the top three for the next two months, before once more returning to the top. By the end of November, "She Loves You" had sold over a million copies. It would be Britain's biggest-selling single of the 1960s.

Earlier in August, with their first album still at the top of the charts, The Beatles took some time out of their busy schedule to record some new material for a second album. Once again, Abbey Road's Studio Two was home for these sessions. This time, instead of rushing through they were

Opposite: Contact sheet with images of The Beatles' London Palladium concert showing police attempting to restrain hoardes of fans, October 13, 1963.

Next spread: Ringo Starr, George Harrison, Paul McCartney and John Lennon perform on *Late Scene Extra*, November 25, 1963.

WING 13 10 63

given a little longer – three days. It was during these sessions that Martin began to realize that there was more to The Beatles than the four charismatic lads that he had first worked with. The band themselves were becoming more at ease with the recording process, increasingly taking a keen interest in how to use the studio most effectively. John in particular wanted to understand new recording techniques. He quickly grew fond of double-tracking the lead vocal, recording the vocal twice and keeping both versions in the mix to bolster the sound of the voice. At the same time, their own songs were gaining in confidence and complexity, their sources of inspiration ever widening.

THE BIRTH OF BEATLEMANIA

An indication of the way pop music was viewed by the media of the day can be seen in The Beatles' first documentary, filmed at the end of August, 1963. BBC producer Don Haworth wanted to make a film about the Merseybeat phenomenon, but rather than shooting a piece full of Liverpool bands, he chose to present it from a sociological perspective. The 30-minute documentary featured The Beatles and other Mersey acts playing and talking, interlocking in an attempt to give the viewer a feel for life in Liverpool. Broadcast at the end of October, *Merseybeat* was both a popular and critical success. In many ways it was the first time the media prepared to concede that pop music was not the exclusive preserve of poorly educated, working-class teenagers. *Merseybeat* is now widely viewed as an important document in the history of British pop culture.

October 1963 saw The Beatles embark on their first European tour – seven dates in Sweden. Not renowned as an important rock 'n' roll market, Sweden was nonetheless The Beatles' first major overseas conquest. The tour began with a broadcast on Swedish national radio. The seven dates that followed produced the sort of audience mayhem that would forever be associated with The Beatles – hordes of screaming teenage girls – and alongside them in the crowd were their boyfriends sporting the band's characteristic "mop top" haircut – amusingly noted in the Swedish press as the "Hamlet style".

Although The Beatles were beginning to get used to the teenage adulation, their return to the UK came as something of a shock. As the plane taxied down the runway at London's Heathrow Airport, the sound of jet engines faded to the roar of hundreds of screaming Beatles fans. The scenes of madness made headline news in the national press, perpetuating the idea that Beatle hysteria was running out of control.

The Beatles couldn't keep out of the headlines now. On Monday, November 4, The Fab Four played what was for many entertainers the truest indication that they had reached the top of their

Left: A flyer for The Beatles performing at the ABC, Huddersfield, November 29, 1963.

Opposite: Queen Elizabeth I talking to The Beatles after the Royal Variety Show, November 4, 1963.

profession – The Royal Command Performance. This was an annual British "showbiz" tradition where a cast of top variety artists – singers, comedians, magicians, acrobats – performed before members of the British Royal family. The show was broadcast on a Sunday night and always received among the highest annual TV audience figures – so much so that, with a spirit of gentlemanly fair play characterizing the early days of British television, the two major networks took it in turns to broadcast the show.

The Beatles caused a sensation in more ways than one. Although clearly nervous, their cheeky humour won over the starchy, conservative, dinner-jacketed audience. Before playing their final number – their usual version of The Isley Brothers' "Twist and Shout" – John made his legendary request for audience participation: "Will people in the cheap seats clap your hands? All the rest of you, if you'll just rattle your jewellery!" The quip was outrageous

in such a deferential environment, and yet its delivery came across as innocent cheek. It could have been very different. Before the show John had joked with Epstein that if the audience were being too subdued he would "just tell 'em to rattle their fuckin' jewellery".

The newspapers couldn't get enough of The Beatles. They reported that both the Queen Mother and Princess Margaret had visibly enjoyed the performance, which was described in a headline by the *Daily Express* – "Beatles Rock The Royals". When she met them after the show, the Queen Mother asked where they were performing next. When she was told they were playing in Slough, Her Majesty mischievously replied, "Oh, that's near us." Reporting on the scenes of mayhem outside The Prince of Wales Theatre, the *Daily Mirror* could find only one word to describe this new phenomenon – "Beatlemania".

DEREK ARNOLD PRESENTS the *BEATLES*

at the

ROYAL HALL
HARROGATE

on

FRIDAY
8th MARCH
1963

SOUVENIR
PROGRAMME

PRICE
1 - 0

also appearing

BARRY CORBETT *AND HIS* MUSTANGS
and the CHINCHILLAS
RICKY FENTON *AND THE* APACHES

Left and below: A programme for The Beatles at the Royal Hall, Harrogate, March 8, 1963.

Opposite: Paul McCartney and George Harrison at rehearsals, 1963.

THE BEATLES STORY

Why the Beatles? To quote John Lennon "It came to us in a vision - a man descended unto us astride a flaming pie and spake these words, unto us, saying 'From this day on you are the Beatles with an A.' Thus it did come to pass thus" The group could be said to have been founded in 1956 when John, Paul, and George met at school. They played together as a group under various names and with various drummers until 1960 when they made a name for themselves playing in a Hamburg night club. On returning they opened as 'The Beatles' at a suburban Town Hall. The reception was rapturous and from there they went from strength to strength untill April 1961 when they were once again invited to play in Hamburg. Their return to Liverpool was met with packed Halls. In November '61 were voted Mersysides most popular group. They have given several radio & T.V. performances. Parlophone Records signed them up early in 1962 and their first single written by Paul and John features "Love me do" and "P.S. I love you" which reached number 17 in the charts. Their follow-up "Please please me" and "Ask me why" shot up the hit parade and reached the top early in March.

GEORGE HARRISON (above)

LEAD GUITAR 19 years of age dislikes having his hair cut and travelling on buses - likes sleeping, girls and driving - educated at Liverpool Institute.

JOHN LENNON (right)

RHYTHM GUITAR - also plays banjo harmonica, maraccas & piano - likes music, books, curries, painting, television & intelligent blondes - 22 years of age - educated at Liverpool College of Art.

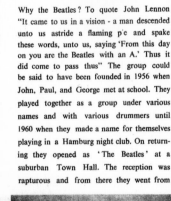
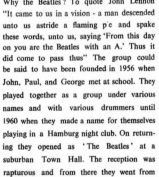

PAUL McCARTNEY (above)

BASS GUITAR - also piano, drums, and banjo - dislikes shaving - likes any type of girl except soft ones - 20 years of age - educated at Liverpool Institute - interested in writing songs and reading.

RINGO STARR (left)

DRUMS - 22 years of age - educated at Dingle Vale Secondary School - was in the same class as Billy Fury hobbies include drums, cars and well built blondes 5 ft. 5 ins. tall.

Presented to
PAUL McCARTNEY
by his friends at
E.M.I. RECORDS LTD
for the best selling E.P.
of all time
AUGUST 1963

DOMINATING BRITAIN

The final two months of 1963 saw an unprecedented level of interest in a group of entertainers. Fleet Street endowed them with front page after front page. In examining the apparent effect The Beatles had on young girls, the *Sunday Times* was first to start drawing sexual parallels. One psychologist, writing for the *News Of The World*, pronounced that the screams of young girls were subconscious preparations for motherhood! The Beatles were even mentioned in Parliament. Finally, despite of all Epstein's attempts to cover it up, the news broke that John was married with a son. Few were overly concerned – it was just another interesting fact in an ongoing saga.

On November 22, 1963, The Beatles' debut album was finally dislodged from the top of the album charts, but only by their follow-up album, *With The Beatles*. Never before had there been such anticipation for a pop LP. Advanced orders of a quarter-of-a-million copies confirmed The Beatles' hold on Britain. The first two albums by the group set a record that no other artist has come near to matching: 50 consecutive weeks at the No. 1 spot – 29 for *Please Please Me* and 21 for *With The Beatles*.

With The Beatles was a pioneering album. The music was notably more sophisticated than its predecessor, showing just how much the band had grown in confidence. Its presentation also set it apart from other pop albums. Although American jazz albums released by labels such as Verve and Blue Note made clear connections between music and art – pop artist Andy Warhol had been responsible for many fine jazz album covers in the late 1950s – such thought rarely went into the artwork used on pop albums. For the jacket of *With The Beatles*, however, Epstein hired one of Britain's top fashion photographers, Robert Freeman, who produced four moody black-and-white portraits, each one split by a shadow. The photographs were arranged artfully on the four quarters of the jacket.

Left: The Beatles proudly parade an assortment of silver discs presented by EMI Records in London to mark sales of *Please Please Me*, November 18, 1963.

Right: A flyer for The Beatles at Winter Gardens, Margate, where the Fab Four would play twice nightly, commencing July 8, 1963.

ARTHUR HOWES PRESENTS

WINTER GARDENS MARGATE
Entertainments Manager: J. D. Green, F.I.M.E.M. Tel. 22795/21348
WEEK COMMENCING
MONDAY, 8th JULY

ON THE STAGE

6.30 **Twice Nightly** 8.45

Britain's Fabulous Disc Stars!
☆ **THE** ☆
BEATLES

"DO YOU WANT TO KNOW A SECRET"
BILLY J. KRAMER
WITH
THE DAKOTAS

DEAN ROGERS | Britain's Brightest Comedy Star **DEREK ROY** | THE **PAN YUE JEN TROUPE**

THE LANA SISTERS

Reserved Seats 8/6 7/- 5/6 Guaranteed Unreserved 3/-
Box Office open daily 10 a.m. to 8 p.m. Telephone: Thanet 22795/21348

— — — — — — — — — CUT HERE — — — — — — — — —
To The Winter Gardens, Margate THE BEATLES SHOW
Please forward.................. seats at.................. for the..................performance
on .... I enclose s.a.e. and P.O./Cheque value..................
NAME..................
ADDRESS..................

Hastings Printing Company, Portland Place, Hastings. Phone 2450

BEETHOVEN

PLEASE PLEASE ME

SAW HER STANDING

FROM ME TO YOU

TASTE OF HONEY

BOYS

SHE LOVES YOU

TWIST AND SHOUT.

Just one week after *With The Beatles* had begun its chart run, a new single was issued. "I Want To Hold Your Hand" was, rather unusually, not lifted from the album – a fact which doubtless contributed to the one million orders that were placed in advance of its release. John and Paul had written the song a few months earlier in the basement of a house in London's exclusive Harley Street. It was actress Jane Asher's family home, and she was Paul's new girlfriend. In time, "I Want To Hold Your Hand" would become the biggest-selling single in the world by a British artist, with sales estimated to be in excess of 15 million copies.

By the end of 1963, The Beatles had overwhelmed the British pop scene and media in a way that had never happened before, and is unlikely to occur ever again. But it was still only Britain and a few like-minded European cousins. Epstein knew that the biggest battle in his gameplan was still to come ... The Beatles had yet to take on America.

Left: Eskilstuna, Sweden 1963 set list on the business card of Neil Aspinall (later CEO of Apple Corps).

Below: The Beatles meet for the first time after their holidays by candlelight at the Star Steak House in Shaftesbury Avenue, London, October 5, 1963.

Opposite: Set list on autographed promo card, 1963.

UK label:
Parlophone PMC 1206/
PCS 3045

Release Date:
November 22, 1963

US label:
Capitol C2-46436-2

Release Date:
February 1987

Producer:
George Martin

SIDE 1

It Won't Be Long (Lennon/McCartney)

All I've Got To Do (Lennon/McCartney)

All My Loving (Lennon/McCartney)

Don't Bother Me (George Harrison)

Little Child (Lennon/McCartney)

Till There Was You (Wilson)

Please Mister Postman (Holland/Bateman/Gordy)

SIDE 2

Roll Over Beethoven (Berry)

Hold Me Tight (Lennon/McCartney)

You Really Got A Hold On Me (Robinson)

I Wanna Be Your Man (Lennon/McCartney)

Devil In Her Heart (Drapkin)

Not A Second Time (Lennon/McCartney)

Money (That's what I want) (Bradford/Gordy)

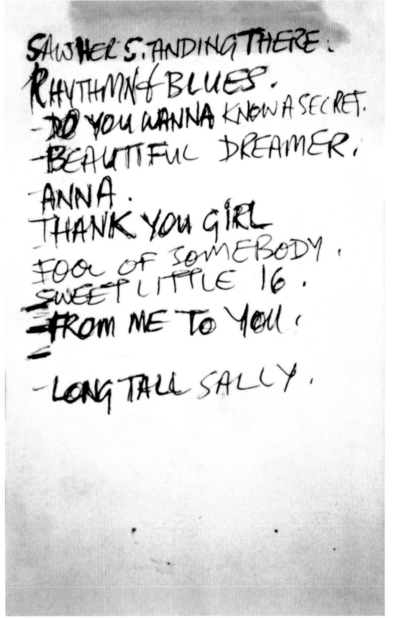

19

6 4

TAKING

AMERICA

EVERYONE KNEW THAT AMERICA HAD INVENTED ROCK 'N' ROLL. THERE WAS ELVIS, CHUCK BERRY, EDDIE COCHRAN, BUDDY HOLLY – THE LIST WAS ENDLESS. THEY HAD CREATED EVERY TREND OF THE PAST TEN YEARS; THEY'D EVEN INVENTED THE TEENAGER. SO WHY ON EARTH WOULD AMERICA CARE ABOUT AN ENGLISH POP GROUP? THAT WAS THE QUESTION THE BEATLES WERE ASKING THEMSELVES AT THE BEGINNING OF 1964.

One might have thought that a contract with a major international record company like EMI – Parlophone's parent label – would immediately open up doors abroad. Especially as EMI already owned the powerful Capitol Records in America. As Parlophone's head of A&R, George Martin was also involved in licensing his label's work overseas. He had sent a copy of "Please Please Me" to his opposite number at Capitol, but the response had not been positive. Eventually Martin, EMI and Epstein settled for a small independent label in Chicago. Although enthusiastic, Vee-Jay Records lacked the resources to provide heavy promotion and the single made little impact. Vee-Jay also released a modified version of the "Please Please Me" album. It went out as *Introducing The Beatles: England's Number One Vocal Group*. England's No. 1 they might have been, but nobody in America was remotely interested.

The situation began to improve when Epstein made his first visit to New York City, ostensibly to license Billy J. Kramer to the famous Liberty label, home of Eddie Cochran's greatest recordings. When Epstein called in on Brown Meggs, Capitol Records director of eastern operations, he brought with him the demo of "I Want to Hold Your Hand" that John and Paul had recorded in Jane Asher's basement. After much deliberation, and given the band's domination of their own country, Capitol finally agreed to give The Beatles a shot.

The ammunition for Brian's onslaught, however, came from a less expected source. Ed Sullivan had a nationwide television show that had launched many a celebrity into the limelight; not least, Elvis Presley himself. While Capitol perhaps failed to grasp the scale of the pandemonium that surrounded The Beatles in Europe, Sullivan had experienced it first hand. Following a trip to Europe, his flight from London's Heathrow Airport had been delayed by the band's heroic return from Sweden. Always on the lookout for new talent, Sullivan was impressed with the impact they had on their fans and saw no reason why their success could not be repeated across the Atlantic. He made Epstein a provisional offer to book them on two of his shows in February 1964. The fee agreed was $3,000, which, unknown to Epstein, was a paltry amount even for a new artist.

Epstein returned to the UK at the end of 1963 to find Beatlemania still in full swing. Critical acclaim was also beginning to erupt. The Beatles won five 1963 Ivor Novello Awards, the most prestigious accolade that the British music business could offer. John and Paul won four of the awards as composers, and in a special fifth award, The Beatles, Epstein and Martin were acclaimed for their "special services to British music".

It was largely Epstein's business acumen that had made The Beatles so successful but it was gradually becoming clear that, although things worked well while he was in control, The Beatles manager was beginning to lose his grip. Quite simply, the whole Beatles phenomenon was becoming bigger than anyone could have ever imagined. Scrupulously fair in his dealings with everyone, Epstein's inexperience in the world of big business would soon begin to let him down. He found that he had less and less time to deal with the minutiae of the band's affairs – the things he did so well – and relied on others, who were less capable, to take care of them on his behalf.

This failing was no more evident than in a series of appalling decisions regarding The Beatles' merchandising arrangements. As a by-product of Beatlemania, all manner of Beatles ephemera began to appear – "mop-top" wigs, Beatles jackets, Cuban-heeled boots, aprons, bedspreads, miniature plastic Beatles guitars ... the list was endless. To begin with, Epstein had personally vetted all products, but this soon became impractical and he handed the task to his lawyer David Jacobs. Pop careers at this time were generally so fleeting that merchandising issues were barely given a thought. Jacobs knew or cared

Previous spread: The boys swimming in a pool in Florida, USA, February 1964.

Opposite: Paul McCartney and John Lennon rehearsing on stage during their tour of America.

Above: The Beatles perform on stage with Ringo hidden behind them, 1964.

GAUMONT - IPSWICH
Manager: P. LOWE
Telephone 53641

ONE DAY ONLY

WEDNESDAY, 22nd MAY at 6.35 and 8.45

Peter Walsh in association with Kennedy Street Enterprises Ltd. and Tito Burns, presents

'PLEASE PLEASE ME'
'FROM ME TO YOU'

THE BEATLES

GERRY and the PACEMAKERS

ERKEY GRANT

IAN CRAWFORD

A Very Good Time for Girls'

DAVID MACBETH

TONY MARSH

TERRY YOUNG SIX

THE LOVELY FAIR AND FEATURES SEAT

LOUISE CORDET

'I'm just a lady'

From the UNITED STATES 'Only the Lonely' 'Dream Baby' 'Running Scared' 'In Dreams'

ROY ORBISON

SEATS   10/6   9/6   8/6   7/6   6/6   5/6

little about the manufacturing business, and so looked elsewhere for assistance. He found it in the form of Nicky Byrne, a well-bred London socialite. He and some friends set up a new company called Seltaeb (Beatles spelt backwards) to exclusively administer the band's merchandising. When negotiating the precise percentage split between NEMs and Seltaeb, Byrne plucked a figure of 90 percent out of the air. To his amazement, Jacobs agreed. Thereafter, NEMS, including The Beatles themselves, would receive just ten percent of the merchandising royalties. At the stroke of a pen a small fortune was signed away.

NEWS FROM THE OTHER SIDE

1964 kicked off with an assault on Paris. France was one of the few European countries yet to yield to rock 'n' roll on a grand scale. The Beatles arrived in France in a blaze of publicity, but for once the great hype machine failed. Firstly there was, and to some extent there still is, a resistance to songs not sung in the French language. Secondly, and more surprising to The Beatles, they were met by a predominantly male audience who were rather less interested in romantic Lennon and McCartney compositions than in straight down-the-line rock 'n' roll. Furthermore, the gigs were plagued by technical difficulties – George's Vox AC30 amplifier was cutting out with such regularity that he began to suspect

that it was being sabotaged. Finally, the all-important French press were less than convinced. While The Beatles would later enjoy success in France, the hysteria never came close to the heights achieved in Britain and America.

In the midst of this minor setback, on January 16, 1964, and completely out of the blue, Epstein received a telegram from Capitol Records in New York. "I Want To Hold Your Hand" had been making steady progress in the lower reaches of the national Billboard charts, but this week it had shot up from No. 43 to the No. 1!

The activity surrounding the single was extraordinary, especially for the large, diverse American market, which was fragmented to such a degree that an artist could be a star on the East Coast and a virtual unknown on the West

Above: A tour poster for The Beatles and Roy Orbison at The Gaumont, Ipswich, May 22, 1963.

Opposite above: Looking at a postcard display on the Champs-Elysees, Paris, 1964.

Opposite below: During a concert at L'Olympia in Paris, January 1964.

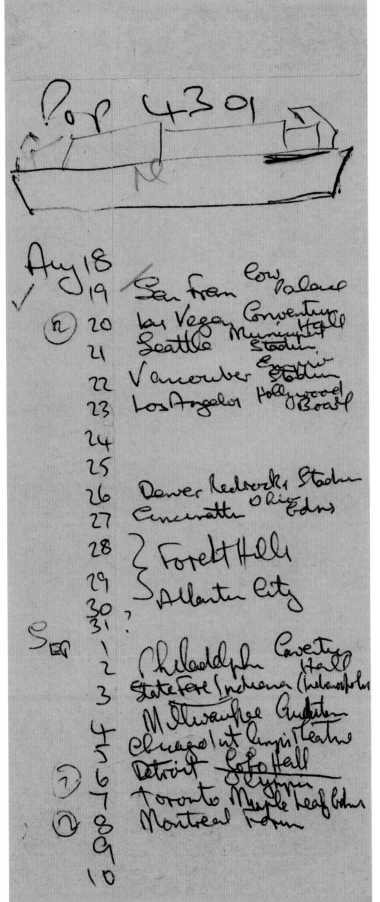

Left: Brian Epstein's itinerary for The Beatles' US tour of 1964.

Right: The Beatles after arriving at John F. Kennedy International Airport, February 7, 1964.

Coast. Stories of extraordinary happenings began to emerge. Radio station WWDC in Washington had obtained a British copy of the single and after a few plays had been besieged by listeners wanting to know more. Similar stories were reported in Chicago and St. Louis. Capitol, bemused by the advanced interest in what they saw as a reluctant low-profile release, seized the opportunity and launched a major publicity campaign. The Beatles were due to arrive in America at the beginning of February and Capitol Records would ensure that people knew it.

To begin with there was a massive "The Beatles Are Coming" poster and windscreen-sticker campaign. Promotional information was circulated to radio stations throughout America along with open-ended interviews, where radio stations received tapes of The Beatles' stock answers to questions recorded in England. The local DJ would then simply re-record the questions, creating the impression of an exclusive interview.

Events leading up to the first appearance on *The Ed Sullivan Show* were fast-moving. The show received over 50,000 applications for the 728 available tickets. Despite this encouraging start, few were prepared to predict that America would succumb to The Beatles' charms in the same way as their fellow countrymen. Nicky Byrne, who had astutely set up a merchandising office in New York, could see the way things were going. He wanted the band to arrive in a magnificent blaze of publicity, but felt that Capitol were still not doing enough. Unable to contact Epstein, Byrne planned his own campaign. He had thousands of T-shirts printed and took out advertisements on two prominent New York radio stations. His offer was a generous one – any teenagers who went to the newly named John F. Kennedy International Airport to greet The Beatles would receive a free T-shirt and a dollar bill.

All of this was unknown to the entourage on board Pan-Am flight 101 as it left London's Heathrow Airport. The Boeing 707 arrived at JFK at 01:20 a.m. on Friday, February 7, 1964 and the sight awaiting The Beatles made the scenes of UK Beatlemania seem tame by comparison. It was truly frightening. As they began to climb down the steps of the plane, they were greeted by 5,000 screaming teenagers. The noise was enough to drown out the rest of the airport. They made their way into the arrivals terminal while a 100-man police cordon held back the surging mass and were led through Customs to an immediate press conference with a 200-strong contingent of New York's media. Clearly dazed but excited by the commotion surrounding them, The Beatles fielded every question – from the most intelligent to the inane – with all the sharp, knockabout "laddish" humour they could muster. When asked if they would be having a haircut while in America, John answered "We had one yesterday." Every one-liner was met with laughter or applause by the gathered media. The Beatles had won their first big battle.

Outside the airport, four chauffeur-driven Cadillac limousines waited to spirit them away to their temporary home – The Plaza Hotel, on New York's famed Central Park. The Beatles had been booked into the hotel a month earlier as a group of "London businessmen". When the hotel owners discovered who they were, they were not pleased. As the absolute antithesis of the clientele for which they usually catered, they tried hard to have The Beatles moved to a different hotel. They were unsuccessful, and the band settled into their suites – the entire twelfth floor of the hotel had been given over to the entourage.

The scenes of hysteria at the airport were reported with a similar air. It was the top national story of the day. Not since war hero General Douglas MacArthur returned from Korea had there been such a public welcome.

UK label:
Parlophone PMC 1230/
PCS 3058

Release Date:
July 10, 1964

US label:
Capitol C2-46437-2

Release Date:
February 1987

Producer:
George Martin

SIDE 1

A Hard Day's Night (Lennon/McCartney)

I Should Have Known Better (Lennon/McCartney)

If I Fell (Lennon/McCartney)

I'm Happy Just To Dance With You (Lennon/McCartney)

And I Love Her (Lennon/McCartney)

Tell Me Why (Lennon/McCartney)

Can't Buy Me Love (Lennon/McCartney)

SIDE 2

Any Time At All (Lennon/McCartney)

I'll Cry Instead (Lennon/McCartney)

Things We Said Today (Lennon/McCartney)

When I Get Home (Lennon/McCartney)

You Can't Do That (Lennon/McCartney)

I'll Be Back (Lennon/McCartney)

Opposite: The Beatles prepare for their Christmas show at the Hammersmith Odeon.

Within the first few days The Beatles received nearly 100 sacks of mail from all over America – Epstein had to set up a small administration department in another hotel to deal with the correspondence.

Two days after their arrival, with George suffering from a severe throat condition, The Beatles made their first ever performance on American soil. The venue was Studio 50 at The Ed Sullivan Theatre on New York's West 53rd Street and Sunday, February 9 was the day when The Beatles conquered America.

After a day of rehearsing and recording material for a later broadcast, *The Ed Sullivan Show* began at 8 p.m. It opened with a dramatic announcement from the host himself: "Yesterday and today our theatre has been jammed with newspapers and hundreds of photographers from all over the nation. These veterans agree with me that this city never has witnessed the excitement created by these four youngsters from Liverpool who call themselves The Beatles. Ladies and Gentlemen ... THE BEATLES!"

A scream erupted from the studio audience. Paul gave a count-in. "1, 2, 3, 4, 5," and the band launched into "All My Loving", quickly followed by "Til There Was You", and "She Loves You". Later in the hour-long programme, they also performed "I Saw Her Standing There" and the band's then-current US No. 1 hit "I Want To Hold Your Hand". As a helpful introduction to the band – as if *any* was really needed – during their second song, the camera gave an individual close-up to each of The Beatles, with a caption showing his name. John's introduction bore an additional line of information: "Sorry girls, he's married!"

The Beatles were visibly thrilled by their reception, but the experience was capped when after their first three songs Ed Sullivan announced that they had just received a telegram from Elvis Presley and Colonel Tom Parker wishing them success on their first visit to America.

This legendary show made television history straight away. The Nielsen Ratings system estimated that *The Ed Sullivan Show* had been watched by 73 million people in 24 million households. In other words, more than 60 percent of all American TV viewers – the world's largest TV audience – had tuned in to watch The Beatles. George said later: "Afterwards they told us that there was no reported crime. Even the criminals had a rest for ten minutes while we were on."

Within a week The Beatles had played high-profile concerts at Washington's Coliseum and New York's prestigious Carnegie Hall. During February 1964, America became besotted with The Beatles. And it stayed that way. Long after the band's acrimonious split, and during the solo careers that followed, it was America more than anywhere else that remained true to the "Fab Four".

When The Beatles left the US at the end of the month they left a continent with an insatiable appetite. The earlier singles released on the small independent Vee-Jay and Swan labels suddenly began selling in enormous quantities. On April 4 1964, this culminated in the total surrender of the Billboard chart. With the top two positions in the album charts filled by The Beatles, the band's singles could be found at numbers 1, 2, 3, 4, 5, 31, 41, 46, 58, 65, 68 and 79. Similarly, in Australia The Beatles took the top six chart positions. No artist in the history of popular music has ever come anywhere near this level of domination.

THE SILVER SCREEN

As ever, Brian Epstein was busy preparing the next phase of his masterplan. But once again, his inexperience with big business would undermine his success. While in America, Nicky Byrne had made almost $100,000 in merchandising. When he presented Epstein with a cheque for the NEMS share, which had been agreed at 10 percent, Brian was pleasantly surprised, before asking how much of it he owed to Byrne! A similar story transpired when The Beatles made their first feature film. Epstein went into negotiations with United Artists with a firm threshold figure of 7.5 percent of the royalties – under no circumstances would he accept anything less. United Artists, meanwhile, had been expecting, and prepared, to pay up to 25 percent. In addition, he signed a deal that committed The Beatles to three films and allowed the rights to revert back to the producer after 15 years. Although the fee was eventually renegotiated, it was more evidence that things were getting out of control. Joe Orton, one of Britain's top playwrights of the 1960s – widely remembered by the public for his dramatic murder in August 1967 – also had his doubts about Epstein. He had been commissioned to create a script for a Beatles film – one that was ultimately never used – but felt that Epstein was certainly not equipped to judge its merits. A Beatles fan himself, Orton states in his published diaries that it is "extraordinary that someone like Epstein has absolutely no idea how valuable a property The Beatles are." It was looking as if Epstein was playing out of his league, unable to comprehend the financial potential of his protegees, but also too closely involved to appreciate their growing cultural significance.

During March and April 1964, Beatlemania had developed a momentum that no longer needed to be continuously stoked by a heavy performing schedule. This period was devoted to making a feature film. Its working title had originally been *Beatlemania*, but it was later dropped in favour of one of Ringo's Liverpudlian phrases – *A Hard Day's Night*. Richard Lester was the director given the task of converting the group's unique humour onto the big screen. Lester was an ideal choice; his best-known work up until that point had been *The Running Jumping & Standing Still Film* (1960), featuring John's radio heroes, The Goons. The script was written by Alun Owen, who had a

reputation based on a number of highly acclaimed gritty television dramas set in Liverpool. It was felt that his knowledge of The Beatles' home city would give a more authentic feel to their dialogue. The producers sensibly steered clear of placing too much performance pressure on The Beatles themselves – after all, they had reached the pinnacle of their profession as musicians, not actors. In fact, nobody had the slightest idea how well they would stand up.

The storyline would be a simple one: The Beatles would play themselves in a series of set-pieces that could easily have come straight from incidents in their own hectic lives.

A Hard Day's Night shows The Beatles in their familiar wisecracking press-conference mode, only extended throughout an entire film. The Beatles were so convincing that many thought that the film really was The Beatles just

Below: A still from The Beatles' movie debut, *A Hard Day's Night*, released on August 11, 1964.

Opposite: Poster for concert at the Kerridge Odeon, Wellington, New Zealand, June 22–23, 1964.

KERRIDGE ODEON *presents the...*

PHENOMENON OF SHOW BUSINESS IN PERSON —

THE BEATLES

Supported by ....

TOWN HALL
MON., JUNE 22nd
TUES., " 23rd
*TWO NIGHTS ONLY—
TWO BIG SHOWS!*

6 P.M. & 8·30

SOUNDS *Incorporated*
6 DYNAMIC INSTRUMENTALISTS FROM BRITAIN —

JOHNNY DEVLIN

THE PHANTOMS
AUSTRALIA'S TOP BACKING GROUP —

JOHNNY CLUSTER AND DEL JULIANNA

BOOK AT THE D.I.C. NOW *!*

BOEING 707 AIRLINER.

POST CARD

CORRESPONDENCE   ADDRESS

playing around and making it up as they went along. In fact, it had been a very tightly scripted film.

The Beatles themselves were a revelation. Bolstered by a sturdy British cast that included Wilfrid Brambell (television's Albert Steptoe) and Shakespearean actor Victor Spinetti, there were few signs of the stilted or wooden performances that marred so many similar projects. All four Beatles played their parts with great confidence, especially Ringo whose performance was singled out by many critics. During a lengthy scene where he "escapes" from the band and walks along the canal on his own he delivers a performance of engaging pathos.

When the film was released in August 1964, the critics were generally in favour. *A Hard Day's Night* proved to be a great success internationally, earning $14 million when it was first released. There were also a number of foreign-language versions released with alternative titles. In Germany, where The Beatles had enjoyed two hits in translation "Komm, Gib Mir Deine Hand" and "Sie Liebt Dich" (bizarrely, perhaps, also hits in the US), the film was issued as *Yeah Yeah Yeah – Die Beatles*. Italians saw the film as *Tutti Per Uno* (All for One), while the French called it *Quatre Garcons dans le Vent* (Four Boys in the Wind).

Naturally, a movie starring The Beatles playing themselves had to have a brand new set of songs and before the cameras started to roll, they spent three days recording new material with Martin at Abbey Road. In addition, as the film's musical director, George Martin also recorded a number of instrumental takes on the same songs.

A Hard Day's Night was the first Beatles' album to contain entirely original contributions. At this time, John was still widely seen as the dominant force in the band, and of the eight Lennon/McCartney compositions used in the film, John was largely responsible for seven of them.

Presentation of The Beatles soundtrack albums always differed between the UK and America. In the UK, the songs from the film appeared in sequence on the first side of *A Hard Day's Night*; the other side featured unrelated new material recorded in June after the movie had been completed. In America, however, it was treated purely as a soundtrack album and featured only the songs in the film. To pad the album out to a respectable length some of George Martin's incidental music – often orchestral versions of the same songs – was inserted.

NOWHERE TO RUN

Having conquered America, The Beatles returned from their month off ready to take on the rest of the world. After a brief spell in Holland and Scandinavia, they flew out to the Far East and Australia. The scenes that greeted them were by now becoming startlingly familiar. On their flight from Hong Kong to Sydney, they made an unscheduled refuelling stop at Darwin in the north of Australia. Even at 2 o'clock in the morning a crowd of 400 fans suddenly appeared out of nowhere to greet The Beatles.

On their return to the UK, The Beatles spent a few days at Abbey Road laying down tracks for yet another new album before jetting off for a second US tour. This time their reception was, if possible, even more hysterical. At San Francisco International Airport, they were carried from the airport in what can only be described as a protective iron crate. This time, they would be playing all over the country and for the event they hired a private Lockheed Electra jet plane to get them from city to city.

By now The Beatles were beginning to realize that they were experiencing something totally unique; something that nobody outside of the band would be able to comprehend. As George said, "I always felt sorry for Elvis because he was on his own – nobody else knew what it felt like to be Elvis, but it was different for us – the four of us shared the experience."

The Beatles stayed in America for just over a month – they played 32 dates in 34 days in 24 cities, created havoc, and then came home. With barely time to slot in overdubs for the new album and record a new "A" side, their incredible workload continued with yet another major British tour.

CHANGING TIMES

The album that followed, *Beatles For Sale*, reflected the chaotic lifestyle in which the four now found themselves. In a short space of time they had all become fabulously rich – wealthy enough to buy a country mansion, and to allow their parents to retire in luxury (with the exception of Ringo's mother Elsie, who steadfastly refused to leave her family home in Liverpool).

But the constant pressure of life on the road began to take its toll on the music. *Beatles For Sale* was a rather tired and disappointing effort that harked back to their old days at The Cavern. Rather than coming up with a complete set of new material, they filled holes by using old rock 'n' roll songs they had been playing for years.

However, one new influence could now be heard in some of the group's new songs. The New York folk scene had produced an influential new voice, a young singer/songwriter named Bob Dylan whose protest songs like "The Times They Are A-Changin'" had become popular anthems for a disaffected American youth. While on tour, The Beatles met Bob Dylan – it was here that they were reputed to have first smoked marijuana. The whole band fell under the spell of Dylan's music.

Among The Beatles' greatest strengths was their open-mindedness to new influences. In spite of the fact that they were the most popular entertainers on the face of the planet, they were nonetheless keen to explore other interesting areas. As George recalled, "We had Dylan's album and we played it over and over again – it gave us a real buzz." Paul was even more enthusiastic: "He was our idol."

It's not hard to understand Dylan's appeal to such craftsmanlike songwriters as Lennon and McCartney – the sparse acoustic backing allowed the lyrics to do the talking. Until this time, The Beatles had concerned themselves with developing their music; the lesson that they, and countless others, learned from Bob Dylan was that it was possible to say something more than just the blindingly obvious or emotionally trite in the context of a pop song.

Beatles For Sale (or *Beatles '65* as it was known in the US), appeared in December of 1964, only four months after their previous album. Despite being a less substantial piece of work, the album went straight to No. 1, replacing

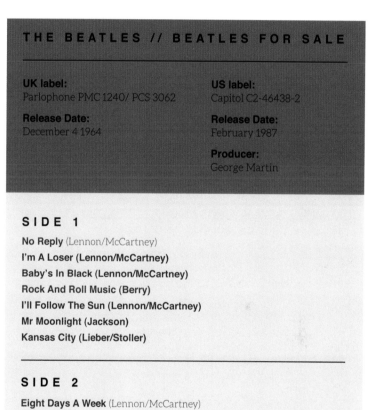

THE BEATLES // BEATLES FOR SALE

UK label:
Parlophone PMC 1240/ PCS 3062

US label:
Capitol C2-46438-2

Release Date:
December 4 1964

Release Date:
February 1987

Producer:
George Martin

SIDE 1

No Reply (Lennon/McCartney)

I'm A Loser (Lennon/McCartney)

Baby's In Black (Lennon/McCartney)

Rock And Roll Music (Berry)

I'll Follow The Sun (Lennon/McCartney)

Mr Moonlight (Jackson)

Kansas City (Lieber/Stoller)

SIDE 2

Eight Days A Week (Lennon/McCartney)

Words Of Love (Holly)

Honey Don't (Perkins)

Every Little Thing (Lennon/McCartney)

I Don't Want To Spoil The Party (Lennon/McCartney)

What You're Doing (Lennon/McCartney)

Everybody's Trying To Be My Baby (Perkins)

A Hard Day's Night at the top of the charts on both sides of the Atlantic. The album went on to sell nearly six million copies across the globe.

By the end of 1964 The Beatles truly had conquered the world, but that year had also taken its toll on the band. Photographs from their run of Christmas performances at London's Hammersmith Odeon show them looking fatigued; John scarcely trying to mask his exhaustion, and even the ever-friendly Paul finding it hard to raise a smile. They had achieved greater success than any other group in history, so where else was there to go now? One thing was certain, it was not a year that they would, or even could, go through again.

Your Invitation to the PRESS SHOW of

"A HARD DAY'S NIGHT"

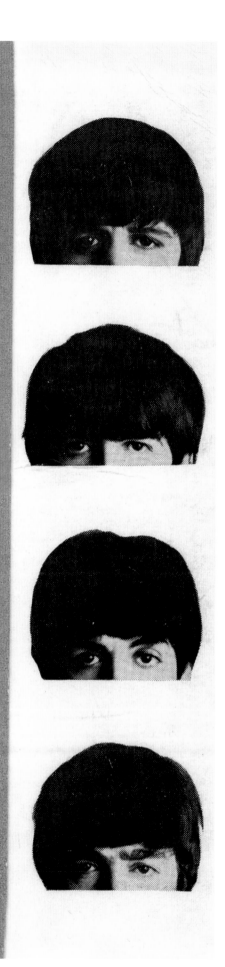

Left: An invitation to the press show of *A Hard Day's Night*.

Right: A programme for The Beatles at the Milwaukee Auditorium, September 4, 1964.

Triangle Theatrical Productions

Franklin Fried PRESENTS

THE BEATLES

Milwaukee Auditorium — Sept. 4 — Milwaukee

1965

FROM

POP

TO

ART

IF 1964 WAS THE YEAR IN WHICH THE BEATLES TOOK ON THE WORLD, 1965 WAS TO BE THEIR PERIOD OF TRANSITION. ALTHOUGH THEY WERE STILL FANTASTICALLY POPULAR, THE BEATLEMANIA PHENOMENON WAS BEGINNING TO SHOW SIGNS OF RUNNING OUT OF STEAM. NONETHELESS, THE BEATLES THEMSELVES WERE STILL UNDER EXTREME PRESSURE TO CONSOLIDATE THEIR REMARKABLE SUCCESS. BRIAN EPSTEIN'S 1965 GAME PLAN WOULD INCLUDE ANOTHER TOUR OF THE US, A SECOND FEATURE FILM AND MORE PERFORMANCES ON BRITAIN AND EUROPE.

But while the great wheels of Epstein's NEMS empire were grinding relentlessly onwards, the four young men at the sharp end were beginning to harbour doubts about the direction in which they were heading. For one thing, they were finding live performances increasingly difficult to take seriously. Whereas they had once prided themselves on being an extremely tight, accomplished group of musicians, nowadays all they could hear when they played was the incessant screaming of teenage girls. Nobody, it seemed, actually came to listen to them anymore. While they made light of it publicly – John would say, "If they want to pay their money to come and scream at us, that's fine by me" – privately they were beginning to feel that it was all rather futile.

Their live performances became increasingly mechanical and, by their own admission, their standard of musicianship was beginning to slip. They had already found to their amusement that any one of the band – even Ringo – could stop playing for a few seconds without anybody noticing. John, who had always jokingly told the screaming fans to "Shaddup!" no longer bothered – he was becoming more inclined to yell obscenities at the audience away from the microphone.

At this point, The Beatles all agreed that they wanted to reduce the amount of time devoted to touring. Instead, they would throw all of their energies into songwriting and mastering the recording process. If 1964 marked The Beatles as the most potent commercial force in music history, then 1965 sowed the seeds of transformation that would eventually see them viewed as being among the greatest artists in the history of popular music.

By the middle of January, after completing the last of their Christmas shows at London's Hammersmith Odeon, The Beatles were able to return to their various newly acquired estates to sort out personal matters and write new material for the soundtrack of their forthcoming second film.

John quickly settled into Kenwood, his Surrey mansion home, with Cynthia and Julian. Although still the most controversial and provocative Beatle, he was a homeboy at heart, who liked nothing more than lounging on the sofa watching television, reading books and magazines, or listening to records. John's appearance had visibly altered more dramatically than any of the others: he suddenly put on weight and his face developed a puffy roundness. Cynthia was happy to interpret this as contentment as night after night, when Julian had been put to bed, the pair would sit around listening to Bob Dylan records.

Paul lived a more social life. He was frequently seen with Jane Asher in tow – or tagging along with her, to be more accurate. Jane's background couldn't have been more different from Paul's: her father was a doctor, her mother a music professor, and their family home was a large townhouse in London's fashionable Wimpole Street. Rather than buy his own property, as the others had done, Paul decided to move into a vacant room at the top of the Ashers' home.

Asher seemed like the perfect girlfriend for the "perfect" Beatle. She was beautiful, intelligent and, most of all, discreet. Their romance was a highly public one that saw the couple continually hounded by the press to "name the day" of their wedding. There was, however, a problem on the horizon. Barely 20 years old, Jane was already establishing herself as a fine young actress, with a number of high-profile roles to her credit. At that time, Paul's working-class upbringing struggled with the idea of having a wife who went out to work. It was a problem that they would never manage to resolve.

In the eyes of the world the "lesser" Beatles – George and Ringo – found themselves under less public scrutiny. They were allowed to go about their relationships with a little more ease. George had become smitten with a young

model named Pattie Boyd whom he had met on the set of *A Hard Day's Night* the previous year. They would be seen hanging out together at London's most fashionable clubs. Later on in the year Boyd would move into *Kinfauns*, George's luxury bungalow set back in a wooded National Trust estate in Esher, Surrey – the heart of England's "stockbroker belt".

From the beginning, Brian Epstein had gone to great lengths to present The Beatles as four young, fun-loving and – above all – *unattached* young lads. Like many a star-maker before him, he felt that an important tactic was to promote the fantasy that any teenage fan, no matter how humble, might just be the one to tie down their chosen Beatle. When The Beatles started to "go public" with their women, the treatment meted out by fans to the Beatle-girls could sometimes be harsh.

Cynthia Lennon was already well-established. She had won her man and started a family, so was accepted fully by the fans as a part of "The Beatle package". Asher (and to lesser extent Boyd) also proved popular because, as actress and model respectively, they were typical aspirational figures for teenage girls. And they were exactly the kind of girlfriends that everyone would wish for and expect of the "Fab Four".

However, young Maureen Cox, just 18, was dealt a much poorer hand. She had been Ringo's girlfriend since he spotted her waiting to see The Beatles at The Cavern. Their relationship had for a long time been a long-distance affair. Even though he, like the other Beatles, was now based in London, she

remained in Liverpool where she worked as a hairdresser. Perhaps it was because she was just a regular local girl that she felt the full venom of the city's teenage girls. Yet at the same time, Cox showed that a teenage fantasy *could* come true: in many ways this made her the most envied of all The Beatles' women.

"WON'T YOU PLEASE HELP ME?"

On Monday, February 15, 1965, The Beatles moved back into what was fast becoming their second home – Studio Two at Abbey Road. With budgets gradually growing commensurate with their popularity, they were given a whole week to come up with a soundtrack album for their new film. This would also hopefully include a couple of hit singles. After that they would have to spend the best part of the next three months back in front of the cameras.

A Hard Day's Night had proved to be more successful – both commercially and artistically – than anyone could have hoped. So, for their second film, United Artists agreed to budget of $1.5 million – three times that of their debut. When the cameras first started rolling, on location in the Caribbean paradise of Nassau in the Bahamas, the film was still provisionally being referred to as *Beatles Two*, although Ringo's wittily surreal suggestion – *Eight Arms To Hold You* – was also used for a time. In the end they settled for *Help!*, after one of the songs that John had written for the soundtrack, which was also under serious consideration as the next single.

Although director Richard Lester was again at the helm, *Help!* was to be an altogether less satisfying experience than its predecessor. There were problems with the script, which was far less successful in capturing the essence of The Beatles dry, laconic, in-joke humour. Its main failing, however, was that the story placed the band outside of their comfort zones: it wasn't about four lads in pop group, but The Beatles in a surreal, comic-book adventure.

The story revolves around a mythical Indian religious cult that discovers their sacrificial ring is missing. It has, in fact, been sent to Ringo by a mysterious fan. Once the hapless drummer places it on his finger he finds it impossible to remove. The Beatles are pursued for the rest of the film by members of the cult – again played by a well-respected cast of top British actors and comedians like Leo McKern, Warren Mitchell, Roy Kinnear, Victor Spinetti and Eleanor Bron – demanding that the ring be returned.

Help! was shot in a variety of exotic locations – from the Bahamas they moved on to Obertauern in the snowcapped Austrian mountains. The overall air of the film was more chaotic than their previous attempt, making the plot, such as it was, difficult to follow in places – the internal logic that director Lester clearly sought was not always apparent. In places *Help!* came close to a parody of a James Bond movie, but, as before, The Goons and the Marx Brothers were the clearest influences. The Beatles, aided no doubt by the constant use of marijuana on the set did loosen up noticeably, and all gave adequate performances. However, as the victim and hero of the film, Ringo once again stood out as the most naturally capable actor.

Although *Help!* was another major commercial success – the biggest-grossing British film of 1965, in fact – cinema critics were this time less forgiving. The Beatles also disliked the film. Asked by a reporter at the time if they could "look forward" to any more Beatle movies, John replied stoically, "Well, there'll be many more but I don't know whether you can look forward to them or not." Later he recalled: "*Help!* was a drag because we didn't know what was happening...we were on pot by then, so the best stuff is on the cutting-room floor, with us breaking up and falling about all over the place."

The following year, with one further film to make to fulfill their contract with United Artists, Brian Epstein approached a young playwright named Joe Orton, who had just made his name in the West End with *Loot*, a scurrilously funny black comedy that had shocked the establishment with its attitude toward death, crime and bisexuality. In the space of a few hectic years between 1965 and 1967, the openly homosexual Orton became the darling of the West End theatre set, embracing the prevailing wind of "Swinging London" as much as any man.

Opposite: Ringo pictured with his wife Maureen at a press conference the day after their wedding, February 12, 1965.

Above: At Cliveden House in Buckinghamshire during the filming of *Help!* in May 1965.

UK label:
Parlophone PMC 1255/
PCS 3071

Release Date:
August 6, 1965

US label:
Capitol C2-46439-2

Release Date:
April 1987

Producer:
George Martin

SIDE 1

Help! (Lennon/McCartney)

The Night Before (Lennon/McCartney)

You've Got To Hide Your Love Away (Lennon/McCartney)

I Need You (George Harrison)

Another Girl (Lennon/McCartney)

You're Going To Lose That Girl (Lennon/McCartney)

Ticket To Ride (Lennon/McCartney)

SIDE 2

Act Naturally (Morrison/Russell)

It's Only Love (Lennon/McCartney)

You Like Me Too Much (George Harrison)

Tell Me What You See (Lennon/McCartney)

I've Just Seen A Face (Lennon/McCartney)

Yesterday (Lennon/McCartney)

Dizzy Miss Lizzy (Williams)

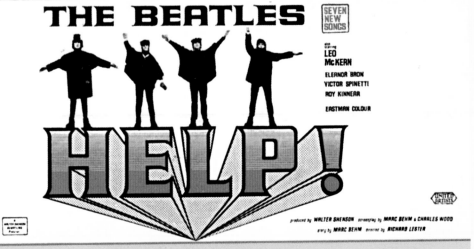

Left: A ticket to The Beatles' performance of *Help!* at London Pavilion, Piccadilly Circus, July 29, 1965.

Opposite: George Harrison recording on a Rickenbacker electric guitar in the studio, circa 1965.

In 1967 Orton was commissioned to write a script for the third Beatles film, and came up with *Up Against It*, a tale that combined the debauched scenarios for which his plays were notorious with a farcical plot to assassinate a female prime minister. Orton had little direct contact with The Beatles or their representatives, but after a long delay the script was evidently returned to him without comment. Orton revised it and had been planning to discuss the project with Richard Lester when, on August 9, 1967, Orton famously met a dramatic death at the hands of his embittered lover and collaborator Kenneth Halliwell.

In the end, *Help!* was to be The Beatles' final foray into the world of movie acting – as a group, at least. They would eventually overcome United Artists' contractual requirements by allowing themselves to be filmed in rehearsal, which resulted in the 1970 tell-all documentary *Let It Be*.

BACK TO THE STUDIO

While the hysteria of 1964 was slowly beginning to calm, the popularity of Beatles music showed few signs of abating. April saw the release of the first fruits of their last trip to Abbey Road – John's influential "Ticket To Ride". An early milestone in pop's gradual transformation into "rock", the track revolves around an instantly memorable riff, played by George on his Rickenbacker guitar, which introduces the song and carries into the verse. Throughout the verse, the riff plays over a driving beat and single-note throbbing bass line. John later called it "one of the earliest heavy metal records ever made". Released in April 1965, "Ticket To Ride" went straight to the top of the charts on both sides of the Atlantic, achieving global sales of nearly three million copies.

After the filming of *Help!*, The Beatles returned to the studio for the customary recording of additional songs for the second side of the soundtrack album. On Monday, June 14, Paul started recording a song that he'd been working for some time. The music had come to him in a dream; the lyrics, however, took longer to refine. With a working opening line that began: "Scrambled eggs, Oh my baby how I love your legs", by the time of the recording the song had transformed into "Yesterday". Although not released as a single in Britain at the time, it has become one of The Beatles' most famous songs. It is also one of the most-recorded songs of all time – with close to 2,000 commercially released cover versions.

Opposite: Posing for a portrait in the studio, circa 1965.

Right and below: Signed postcard from *Help!* filming, 1965.

„Hotel Edelweiß", Obertauern, 1738 m
Haus ersten Ranges, Almbar, Teehalle,
Schwimmbad, Sauna, Sonnenterrasse,
geheizte Garagen, ganzjährig geöffnet -
Tel. 0 64 66 - 245

Echte Farbaufnahme — Sturm-Photo, Salzburg-Zürs

Bis zu
5 Grußworten
verbilligtes
Porto

The recording of "Yesterday" was also groundbreaking. George Martin suggested that such a beautiful song should be given a delicate arrangement. Instead of using the band, he hired a string quartet to accompany Paul and a solo acoustic guitar. This was a revolutionary approach to the arrangement of pop music. Just as it is impossible to estimate the impact The Beatles made on the path of popular music, it is also impossible to underestimate Martin's influence on the development of The Beatles.

Although few would doubt that The Beatles would still have gone on to enjoy some kind of success, had Martin chosen not to sign them to his label, it was the way in which he nurtured their burgeoning talents that would play such a major part in the creation of their greatest music. One important reason for this success was simply mutual respect: right from the beginning, Martin

strove to create the feeling that they were all working together for a "greater good". He easily could have told The Beatles what he wanted to do – he was, after all, in a position of power. But he allowed them to explore and learn for themselves, only stepping in when he thought he could achieve the things that they wanted.

For his editorial intelligence alone Martin is widely viewed as pop's premier producer. However, as The Beatles' music became increasingly ambitious, his role in the group became ever-greater. It was he who taught the band the importance of arrangement; added his superior piano skills to many of their records; used his formal music school training to arrange and conduct orchestras; and ultimately showed The Beatles (and the rest of the world) how the recording studio could be treated almost as an instrument in its own right. In his quietly authoritative way, Martin was able to control the potential excesses of the era. No matter how openly rebellious or controversial the band became in public or to one another, they always treated Martin with reverence. Martin, for his part, seemed happy just to be working in the background and, while The Beatles became multi-millionaires, Martin, during his time recording the band, remained simply a salaried member of staff at EMI.

At the end of July, within the space of two weeks, *Help!* the film, the album and the single were all unleashed on the public. All three went to straight to the top of their respective charts.

JOINING THE ESTABLISHMENT

A month before *Help!* was released, The Beatles found themselves at the centre of a rather unexpected controversy. Since October 1964, the prevailing political wind of Great Britain had undergone a radical change in direction. After 13 years under the rule of the Conservative Party, a dynamic young former academic captured the imagination of the country's voters, confidently describing an expanding Britain "forged in the white heat of technological revolution." Harold Wilson's Labour Party was especially popular with young voters, and – unlike any other politician before him – he was keen to embrace popular culture.

On June 12, the Queen's Official Birthday, came the annual announcement of those people who would receive official honours. Traditionally this list was personally drawn up by the Prime Minister and sanctioned as a formality by Her Majesty. Typically, it consisted of military men, politicians, civil servants and businessmen. This year's list included four unexpected names: each one of The Beatles was to receive the MBE – The Membership of the Most Excellent Order of the British Empire.

The popular press were beside themselves – headlines like "She Loves Them, Yeah! Yeah! Yeah!" reflecting the popular triumph. There were also some who were less than happy about a group of pop musicians being honoured in such a way. One outraged naval hero, Colonel Frederick Wagg, returned 12 medals while former RAF squadron leader Paul Pearson returned his MBE because, he felt "it had become debased."

John was initially baffled: "I thought you had to drive tanks and win wars to get an MBE." But he became irritated when the protesters began returning their medals. As far as he was concerned, army officers were given the award for killing people: "We got ours for entertaining. On balance I'd say we deserve ours more." (In 1969, he would return the medal in protest at the British government's foreign policy in Africa.)

The investiture took place at Buckingham Palace on October 26. Outside the Queen's official London residence, 4,000 screaming fans – chanting

Below: The Beatles show off their MBE medals after their investiture at Buckingham Palace, October 26, 1965.

Opposite: George Harrison gives the thumbs up sign on his way to Buckingham Palace.

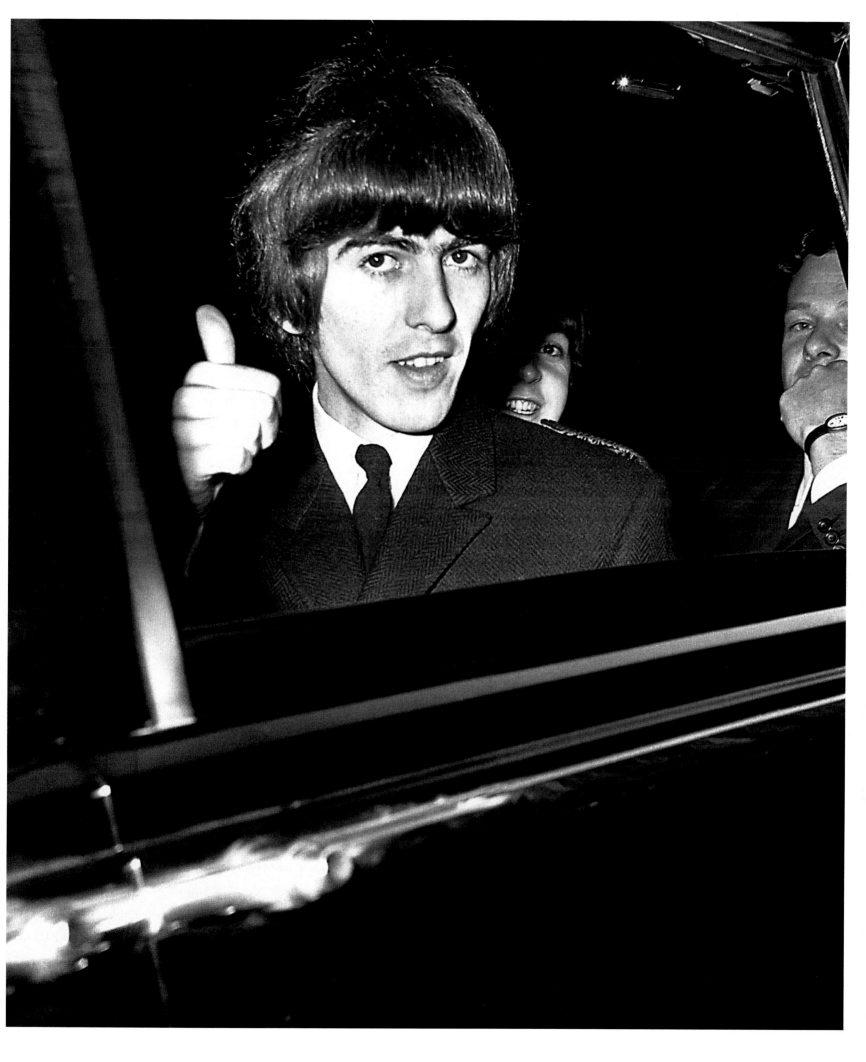

"Long Live The Queen! Long Live The Beatles!" – were held back by a heavy police cordon. The event also gave rise to another of the great Beatles myths. In 1970, French Magazine *L'Express* interviewed John, who claimed that The Beatles had all smoked marijuana in the toilets of Buckingham Palace before the ceremony. This would seem to have been simply a case of John making mischief as the others strenuously denied that it ever took place.

During the ceremony, and at the press conference afterwards, The Beatles kept up their quirky public face. When the Queen asked Paul how long they'd been together, Ringo chipped in "Forty Years." Outside, waving their silver crosses in front of the assembled press, Paul told them that the Queen "was like a mum to us," and that Buckingham Palace was a "keen pad".

THE ACID HOUSE

As with many other pop stars of the period, the use of illicit drugs began to play an increasing role in the lives of The Beatles. One evening, George and Pattie invited John and Cynthia to a dinner party given by a friend. John would later refer to him as a "middle-class London swinger". After enjoying dinner they all retired to the drawing room. There, waiting for them were four small sugar lumps arranged in a line on the mantelpiece. Coffee was served, and their host dropped a lump of sugar into each of their cups. After they had drunk the coffee he advised them not to leave.

Pandemonium ensued. Everyone panicked. They quickly escaped and underwent an unusual trawl of London's nightspots. Cynthia remembered: "The room seemed to get bigger and bigger. Our host seemed to turn into a demon. We got away somehow in George's Mini, but he came after us in a taxi. It was like having the Devil follow us in a taxi." John also remembered the journey: "We were going about ten miles an hour but it seemed like a thousand, and Pattie was saying, 'let's jump out and play football.'" They finally made it back to George's house, but strange things were still happening. By now, John was enjoying the experience: "God, it was terrifying, but it was fantastic. I did some drawings at the time ... of four faces saying 'We all agree with you.' George's house seemed to be like a big submarine, and I was driving it."

They had been given their first acid trip. Acid, or lysergic acid diethylamide (LSD), to give its full name, was the latest drug to hit London. A powerful hallucinogen, LSD had been developed in the 1950s and was widely used on mental patients. However, it had been quietly growing in popularity as a leisure drug among American intellectuals such as the outspoken Harvard teacher Dr Timothy Leary. Within two years, use of LSD would become widespread in alternative circles – the impact it had on the culture of the latter half of the 1960s is quite incalculable.

During the following year, John and George became heavily involved with the drug, although it was John who found it the most profound experience.

Many of his songwriting contributions to The Beatles over the coming two years have the word "acid" written over them in very large and brightly coloured letters. It was much later before Paul and Ringo attempted the drug. Paul was particularly negative: "I don't recommend it. It can open a few doors but it's not any answer. You get the answers yourself." Later, John recalled Paul's reactions: "I think LSD profoundly shocked him, and Ringo. I think maybe they regret it."

BACK TO AMERICA

Only days after the premiere of *Help!* The Beatles hit America for a third time. While their departures and arrivals were now creating slightly less havoc than before, the tour ahead proved that they were still capable of record-breaking feats. After an obligatory recording for Ed Sullivan, Sunday, August 15 saw their momentous concert at the William A. Shea Municipal Stadium, home of the Mets baseball team in New York City. As the concert and surrounding events were being turned into a television film, it was planned to make The Beatles' entrance as dramatic as possible. The original idea was to have the band flown into the stadium by helicopter but this was rejected by the NYC authorities as potentially dangerous. Instead, the group left their hotel in a limousine and drove to a helipad along the Hudson river. From here they flew onto the roof of the World's Fair building – only a few hundred metres

from the stadium – and completed their journey in an armoured truck. At 16 minutes past nine, to the deafening screams of over 55,000 fans, The Beatles sprinted through the players' tunnel, climbed the steps onto the stage, plugged in their guitars, and launched into the opening riff of "Twist and Shout".

As the first concert on the tour, The Beatles were swept along by the magnificent spectacle and gave a performance of startling energy that, happily, was captured on film. *The Beatles At Shea Stadium* captures not only the band giving fine performances of their greatest hits, but the very essence of Beatlemania: the fan hysteria; the expressions on the faces of the teenage girls veering between extreme pleasure and extreme pain; the sheer disbelief that they were in the same location as their idols.

The Shea Stadium concert represented the absolute pinnacle of The Beatles as public performers. The crowd of 55,600 fans was at that time the largest

Previous spread: Fans try to break through a police line at Buckingham Palace where the group were due to receive a MBE.

Opposite: The Beatles perform in front of 56,000 people at Shea Stadium, New York City, August 15, 1965.

Above: The band answer questions regarding their Shea Stadium concert at a press conference in New York City, August 23, 1965.

ever assembled for a pop concert, the box office receipts – $304,000 – were the highest of all time, as was The Beatles' own share of the takings – $160,000.

The rest of the tour, however, lacked the sparkle of the opening triumph. The Beatles quickly lost interest and were now actively beginning to hate being on tour. It didn't matter where they went, the routine was identical: airport arrival; police convoy; hotel room; police convoy; stadium; police convoy; hotel room; police convoy; airport departure. It was with some relief that on September 1, the day after their final US date of the tour in San Francisco, they returned home to a six-week break.

This would be no relaxing holiday for John and Paul though. The group was still contractually obliged to record a new album before the end of the year. Now less inclined to write new material on tour, and wanting more time to produce work of a higher quality, they found themselves having to come up with 12 new numbers for the latest album. Despite the pressure, the new album, *Rubber Soul*, turned out to be their strongest to date.

George Martin saw it as the band's transitional album: "It was the first album to present a new, growing Beatles to the world." Everything about it was just that little bit better than its predecessor. There was also an exploration of new sounds – Paul's "fuzz" bass effect, George's growing love affair with all things Indian, and the first uses of tape manipulation – in the form of Martin's double-speed piano – that would later play such a prominent role in their recordings.

However, it was still John who seemed to be making the most interesting moves. Compositions like "Norwegian Wood (This Bird Has Flown)" show that, still infatuated with Bob Dylan, his lyrics were becoming more personal, even confessional. Similarly "Nowhere Man" with its rich vocal harmonies and sophisticated arrangement seems to be a declaration of the directionless lack of faith, and even boredom, with which he was beginning to view his life.

The sleeve was also a major departure. Along with the psychedelic swirls that make up the album's title, the band, photographed through a "fish-eye" lens, are no longer the four "mop-tops" of old, but four reflective (perhaps even stoned) long-haired young men. Finally, as almost everybody in the civilized world recognized these four faces as easily as any film star or head of state, there didn't even seem to be any real need to mention that it was an album by The Beatles.

On December 3, The Beatles celebrated two new releases. Not only was *Rubber Soul* presented to the world, but a new single – John's "Day Tripper" backed with Paul's "We Can Work It Out". This was a particularly bold move by Parlophone in that both sides of the single were given equal status – it was a "double A-side". More unusually, though, the two songs were not featured on the album. As was by now the tradition, the single went straight to the top of the charts where it remained until the New Year. It was similarly successful across the Atlantic, and went on to sell around three million copies throughout the world.

Rubber Soul was the first Beatles album to be given a serious critical thumbs-up. The public, of course, still needed very little convincing. It became The Beatles' fifth consecutive album to enter the charts at the No. 1 in Britain, where, like the single, it stayed for well into the New Year. In America it broke all records, selling 1.2 million copies within nine days.

Opposite: Beatles fans scream for the band during the concert at Shea Stadium, August 15, 1965.

Right: The boys pose for a portrait, circa 1965.

THE BEATLES // RUBBER SOUL

UK label:
Parlophone PMC 1267/ PCS 3075

US label:
Capitol C2-46440-2

Release Date:
December 3, 1965

Release Date:
April 1987

Producer:
George Martin

SIDE 1

Drive My Car (Lennon/McCartney)
Norwegian Wood (Lennon/McCartney)
You Won't See Me (Lennon/McCartney)
Nowhere Man (Lennon/McCartney)
Think For Yourself (Harrison)
The Word (Lennon/McCartney)
Michelle (Lennon/McCartney)

SIDE 2

What Goes On (Lennon/McCartney/Starkey)
Girl (Lennon/McCartney)
I'm Looking Through You (Lennon/McCartney)
In My Life (Lennon/McCartney)
Wait (Lennon/McCartney)
If I Need Someone (Harrison)
Run For Your Life (Lennon/McCartney)

1966

JESUS,

THE

BUTCHERS

AND THE

PRESIDENT'S

WIFE

THE BEATLES

**MANILA, PHILIPPINES
RIZAL MEMORIAL
FOOTBALL STADIUM
JULY 4, 1966**

FOR THE FIRST THREE MONTHS OF 1966 IT WAS ALL QUIET ON THE BEATLES FRONT. IN FACT, IT WOULDN'T BE UNTIL MAY THAT THEY ACTUALLY PLAYED LIVE AGAIN – BY FAR THEIR LONGEST BREAK SINCE THE DAYS OF THE QUARRY MEN. THE BEATLES STEPPED BACK INTO THEIR (RELATIVELY) ORDINARY LIVES. ON APRIL 6, THEY ONCE AGAIN CONGREGATED AT ABBEY ROAD TO BEGIN WORK ON ALBUM NUMBER SEVEN. THIS TIME THEY WORKED SOLIDLY IN THE STUDIO FOR ALMOST THREE MONTHS – AN UNHEARD-OF EXTRAVAGANCE IN THOSE DAYS.

Magazines and newspapers speculated on what The Beatles could be up to. And well they might.

However, if The Beatles were beginning to enjoy this new lifestyle, June 1966 would soon jolt them back into reality with three absolute nightmare months. It all began well enough. The first fruits of The Beatles' epic studio stay were issued. Paul's "Paperback Writer" was released as a single. Again moving away from the standard love themes, he came up with a song that took the form of a letter written from a would-be author to a potential publisher. Naturally it topped the charts the world over.

Things then started to go wrong with the release in the US of a compilation album, *Yesterday And Today*, containing album tracks that were not used on the US pressings of *Help!*, *Rubber Soul* and their forthcoming masterpiece *Revolver*. All of The Beatles' US albums up to this point had been scaled down versions of their British counterparts, leaving spare tracks to make up new money-spinning albums. This hadn't bothered the band in the past, but the most recent albums had been conceived as complete packages and, although they were powerless to prevent it happening, they were becoming irked by Capitol's uninvited artistic interference. But while *Yesterday And Today* seemed no more than another American rip-off album, The Beatles had no idea at all of the chaos that was currently surrounding the release at Capitol headquarters.

Yesterday And Today was planned to appear in a jacket created at The Beatles' request by British photographer Robert Whitaker. The scene depicted the Fab Four, with huge grins on their faces and wearing white butcher's smocks, covered in slabs of raw meat and mutilated dolls. Production of the album went ahead as planned until, a week before its release date, Capitol was inundated with complaints about the offensive nature of this photograph. After an emergency meeting Capitol decided that it should be withdrawn. At great expense, label staff spent the weekend prior to release replacing the old sleeve with a less "offensive" picture of the band standing around a large suitcase.

The Beatles themselves were completely baffled by the controversy: the photograph had already been used extensively in the British press to promote "Paperback Writer" with no apparent reaction at all. It was clearly a transatlantic cultural quirk. Despite taking the American No. 1 spot, *Yesterday And Today* has the unique honour of being the only Beatles record to make a loss – the repackaging fiasco was said to have cost Capitol an additional $200,000.

THE PHILIPPINES ADVENTURE

In comparison, July seemed likely to be a fairly harmless month. Once again, under duress from Brian Epstein, The Beatles were forced out on the road. Following a few nondescript concerts in Europe, they flew on to play their first-ever dates in Japan. Their arrival in Tokyo created chaos. Leaving the plane at Haneda Airport, they were greeted by 1,500 fans – to The Beatles it was now an unwelcome déjà vu. The Japanese authorities were not used to this kind of behaviour from their young people, and the police were unusually heavy handed in dealing with the crowds. The Beatles had been used to police protection, but nothing like this. Wherever they went they were surrounded by guards: a total of 35,000 security men were employed throughout their three-day stay.

During each of their shows at the Nippon Budokan – already a controversial choice of venue as it was deemed by many to be sacred – the audience of 10,000 had to contend with over 3,000 policemen. Throughout their stay in Japan, The Beatles were "imprisoned" in their suite at the Tokyo Hilton. Armed policemen stood at every possible entrance. The Beatles managed to break out

Previous spread: Arriving back at Heathrow airport following their Far East tour ending in Manila, July 1966.

Opposite: Programme from Rizal Memorial Football Stadium, Manila, July 4, 1966.

to view Tokyo for themselves but were quickly rounded up and returned to the hotel. When John managed to go walkabout early one morning the police threatened to withdraw their services completely. Yet this mayhem was only a dress rehearsal for what was about to happen on the next leg of the tour.

On Sunday, 3 July, The Beatles flew on to play two shows at a football stadium in Manila, the capital city of the Philippines. The local newspapers had helped to create an air of anticipation, with stories of how President Marcos and his family were to be guests of honour at the concerts, and how The Beatles had been invited to visit Mrs Imelda Marcos at Malacañang Palace the following morning. The only problem was that nobody had mentioned this to The Beatles' management. The morning after their concerts, a palace official came to pick them up, only to be told by Epstein that they were all still sleeping and that under no circumstances could they be disturbed. They had unwittingly created an international incident. The newspaper headlines screamed out the great insult – "Imelda Stood Up". It appeared as if the first family of the Philippines had been snubbed. All hell was let loose – their hotel and the British embassy were soon besieged by bomb threats, and the local promoter refused to pay them the receipts from the concerts.

The following day, with the controversy still in full swing, The Beatles prepared to make their getaway. Suddenly, however, they began to find themselves victims of every petty bureaucracy imaginable. They were first told that they couldn't leave the country until they had paid income tax on

their receipts for the concert – but they still had not been paid. After much discussion, Epstein settled the bill just so they could get out of the country as quickly as possible. This was to prove easier said than done. Since the row had broken out, all security had been withdrawn. The Beatles made their way to the airport, all the while being kicked and jostled by angry Filipinos. Having boarded the plane, The Beatles were then told there were irregularities with their documentation: for more than an hour the plane was held up while the correct paperwork was filed. Angry and exhausted, and wondering why they had to continue doing these tours, they were finally able to leave. When they returned to London, a reporter asked George what their next move would be. Already dreading the impending US tour, his weary response was, "We're going to have a couple of weeks to recuperate before we go and get beaten up by the Americans." Little did he know...

A MATTER OF CONTEXT

When celebrities or politicians talk to the press they are always at risk of the interviewer picking out a quote which, when removed from its original context,

Above: The Beatles pose for photographs upon arrival to the Tokyo International Airport on June 29, 1966.

Opposite: John Lennon at a press conference following the group's return from Manila, June 26, 1966.

can take on a very different meaning. This is even more likely to happen when the subject is a young man well known for delivering witty or sarcastic one-liners with a completely straight face. Such a misunderstanding can hardly have exploded with as much force as it did for John at the end of July 1966.

Earlier in the year, John had given an interview to The Beatles' old friend Maureen Cleave of the London *Evening Standard*. During the course of their conversation, John talked about his interest in religion, with the remark, "Christianity will go. It will vanish and shrink. I needn't argue with that...We're more popular than Jesus now."

The interview was published with barely an utterance from the British public. Nearly six months later, on July 19, an American teenage magazine published Cleave's interview under the headline banner: "I don't know which will go first – rock and roll or Christianity." The quote caused a storm and was immediately reported throughout the country. The hard-line American church-goers did not let this pass. Radio station after radio station, especially in the Southern Bible Belt states, banned The Beatles' music. Some went even further, organizing public burnings of Beatles' records and magazines. As ever, John was thoroughly bemused by the American reaction. How was it that so many people could have been so upset by the views of a pop singer?

The Beatles arrived in America on Thursday, August 11 and immediately held a press conference at the Astor Towers in Chicago. As if they could have thought otherwise, the congregated media only wanted to talk to one Beatle. John explained what he had really meant. In fact, he explained it several times, but all they wanted to know was if he was prepared to retract his words. With a puzzled expression and as good a grace as he could muster under the circumstances, John apologized. Then, as quickly as the incident had flared up, the matter was more or less forgotten, and the tour went ahead.

A NEW ART FORM

The Beatles were still battered and bruised from their Far Eastern jaunt, and trying desperately to charge themselves up, with the greatest reluctance, to take on America once again. However, in the midst of the gloom that permeated The Beatles' camp, August 5, 1966 saw a new milestone. Before leaving for America there was one important development to see through. The fruits of three months spent at Abbey Road were about to hit the streets.

Packaged somewhat inauspiciously in a black-and-white sleeve designed by their old friend from Hamburg, Klaus Voormann, *Revolver* represents for many young modern-day fans the moment when The Beatles' story really kicks off. Compared to the songs they were writing just a few months earlier, *Revolver* (an earlier working title of *Abracadabra* having been abandoned) represents a quantum leap forward.

The Beatles had reached such heights of popularity that they were now divorced from all notions of normality. Just being a Beatle meant that they couldn't do things that a normal group of working class lads in their mid-twenties usually do – not without creating a public disturbance, anyway. As individuals, they now moved in more sophisticated circles, and their preoccupations changed.

As Paul said in an interview earlier that year, "We've all got interested in things that never used to occur to us ... I've got thousands of new ideas." So it was under the influence of the fledgling hippie underground, LSD, electronic music, experimental cinema and the avant garde art scene that a new direction gradually began to emerge. The Beatles, being The Beatles, simply dragged the rest of the pop world along in their wake.

The differences that *Revolver* brought to the world of pop music were manifold. For one, it was an album born of studio experimentation – many of the songs were created in the studio, the recording process itself shaping the final compositions. There was also little or no thought given to how it would be possible to perform such pieces in a concert environment. And the songs had changed – as writers, Lennon and McCartney had become "serious". They were producing music for a whole new audience – hip, culturally aware young people, no longer teenage girls.

But most of all, it seemed as if they were now working to please themselves. Although they were all so rich that they could easily have retired and lived the rest of their lives in luxury, they still had one thing to achieve: to be taken seriously as artists. If their old audience could follow them – great; if not, too bad.

Revolver also saw the true birth of the pop album as a coherent body of work, not just a selection of songs thrown together. While the world has long since revised its perception of pop music as an art form – at the time few would have seriously regarded something as radical as Elvis Presley's Sun label recordings as art – *Revolver* was perhaps the first album by a pop group to be treated as a

THE BEATLES // REVOLVER

UK label:
Parlophone PMC 7009/
PCS 7009

Release Date:
August 5, 1966

US label:
Capitol C2-46441-2

Release Date:
April 1987

Producer:
George Martin

SIDE 1

Taxman (George Harrison)
Eleanor Rigby (Lennon/McCartney)
I'm Only Sleeping (Lennon/McCartney)
Love You To (George Harrison)
Here, There And Everywhere (Lennon/McCartney)
Yellow Submarine (Lennon/McCartney)
She Said She Said (Lennon/McCartney)

SIDE 2

Good Day Sunshine (Lennon/McCartney)
And Your Bird Can Sing (Lennon/McCartney)
For No One (Lennon/McCartney)
Dr. Robert (Lennon/McCartney)
I Want To Tell You (George Harrison)
Got To Get You Into My Life (Lennon/McCartney)
Tomorrow Never Knows (Lennon/McCartney)

It has been a pleasure to have you on board. We hope you will like this small memento of your trip with Cathay Pacific, and that you will join us again.

キャセイ航空をご利用下さいまして誠にありがとうございます。このご旅行が良い思い出となり、再びキャセイ航空をご利用下さいますよう心からおまちしております。

留 念 愉 快 的 旅 程
希 望 在 不 久 的 將 來 再 為 君 服 務

CATHAY PACIFIC AIRWAYS

serious work of art. With *Revolver*, The Beatles paved the way for a whole new direction in pop music.

In spite of this evident change in direction, *Revolver* showed that there were still enough fans to take it straight to No. 1, both in Britain and America. In 1966, it went on to sell well over two million copies throughout the world. *Revolver* also showed the extent to which The Beatles were being viewed by their peers, being possibly the most covered album in pop history – six of the songs were released as singles by ten different artists before the album had even come out.

ENOUGH IS ENOUGH

Despite this new flush of critical acclaim, The Beatles still found they had to go back to their old jobs – grinning on stage in front of screaming schoolgirls. Now back in the US with John's Jesus quip just about behind them, The Beatles' third US tour was being executed with all the good grace of a group of bored schoolchildren. Instead of taking the opportunity to showcase tracks from *Revolver*, now widely viewed as one of the greatest albums ever made, they chose to go through the motions, churning out the old material their fans wanted to hear. It all seemed a rather underwhelming exercise. They were playing the same venues as the previous year, but by now Beatlemania was a thing of the past.

They knew they had reached a plateau of popularity: the last thing they wanted was to repeat the process year after year with increasingly diminishing returns. Whatever their fans wanted, The Beatles had changed; simultaneously hitting an all-time high as recording artists, and an all-time low as performers. They didn't even bother rehearsing for the tour. They simply grinded through their half-hour set, played all the old hits until their final show on the August 29. The venue was Candlestick Park in San Francisco. There was nothing remotely unusual about their performance. At 10 o'clock that evening, they

KYA RADIO 1260
WELCOMES
THE BEATLES

RINGO   JOHN   PAUL   GEORGE

AT CANDLESTICK PARK - SAN FRANCISCO
MONDAY AUGUST 29, 1966 - 8:00 P.M.
BLEACHERS ADMISSION $4.50 • NO REFUNDS

PRESIDENT AND GENERAL MANAGER OF KYA
BLEACHERS ADMISSION $4.50

908

THE ≠ BEATLES
BEA TLES

George Harrison
John Lennon
Paul McCartney
Ringo Starr

Odeon
RECORDS

日本航空

世界のアイドル ビートルズ 待望の日本公演!!

6月30日 7月1日 7月2日
6:30開演
日本武道館

A 2,100 / B 1,800 / C 1,500
《全指定席》

主催―読売新聞社・中部日本放送
協賛―ライオン歯磨・ライオン油脂＼後援―日本航空・東芝音楽工業

1501
RIZAL MEMORIAL FOOTBALL STADIUM
MANILA

THE BEATLES

July 4, 1966 — 4:00 P.M.

THE BEATLES

₱20.00   Section BB

                                  Row   9
FIELD RESERVED   Seat   40

came off the stage having played a 33-minute set as uninspired as any of the others on the tour to the usual ecstatic audience reaction. And they would not set foot on another stage again. Ever.

When The Beatles returned to London, everyone, Epstein included, knew that things were going to be different from then on. They made no immediate plans to record again for three months. The lay-off affected each member differently. John immediately distanced himself from the others, disappearing to locations in Germany and Spain to play a role in Richard Lester's new film production, *How I Won The War* (1967). During the long breaks between filming, John would become increasingly bored, occasionally putting pen to paper with some unspecified Beatles project in mind. Neither the film nor John's performance gained many plaudits.

Paul, on the other hand, jumped with typical enthusiasm into London's underground movements. He told the *Evening Standard*, "People are saying things and painting and writing things that are great – I must know what people are doing." His musical activities continued unabated. He took his first tentative steps toward production work – Cliff Bennett and Peter and Gordon, the latter duo featuring Jane Asher's brother – both found success with his support. At the same time he also scored his first feature film, a minor British comedy called *The Family Way* (1966).

George, always the dark horse of the band, had quietly been hating every second of Beatledom throughout the past year. He now considered himself to be a serious musician, and much of what he had endured as a touring Beatle had become demeaning. It was at a dinner party earlier in 1966 that George first met Indian sitar virtuoso Ravi Shankar. While in England, Shankar agreed to visit George for some private tuition. The end of the US tour offered too great an opportunity to miss – George and Pattie disappeared to India for two months. During that time, he studied continuously under Shankar, met with his spiritual advisor, and immersed himself in Indian culture and religion. By the time of their return to England, the Beatle who had shown even less appetite for schoolwork than John – and that was saying something – developed an insatiable appetite for books on yoga, meditation and all things Indian.

Only Ringo seemed to have achieved anything approaching satisfaction with his life. Whenever The Beatles were due to perform he would turn up and do his bit, but otherwise he seemed more than happy to disappear into the luxury of his Sunny Heights estate to be with wife Maureen and their new arrival, a son whom Ringo christened Zak.

The Beatles resumed business on Thursday, November 24, as ever at Studio Two in Abbey Road, and with the ever-present George Martin at the controls. Despite their new personal interests tugging each of them in very different directions, The Beatles remained fiercely loyal to one another. Each of them knew, despite the different frustrations they were experiencing as a Beatle, that there were still only three other people anywhere in the world who could possibly empathize.

Opposite top: A ticket to The Beatles' final full concert at Candlestick Park, August 29, 1966.

Opposite middle: Flyer from The Beatles' Japan tour, 1966.

Opposite below: Ticket for concert at Rizal Memorial Football Stadium, Manila, July 4, 1966.

Above: John Lennon and Paul McCartney share a microphone during the last concert on their final tour.

Above and opposite: John, Ringo and George arrive at the
EMI studios in Abbey Road, London, November 24, 1966.

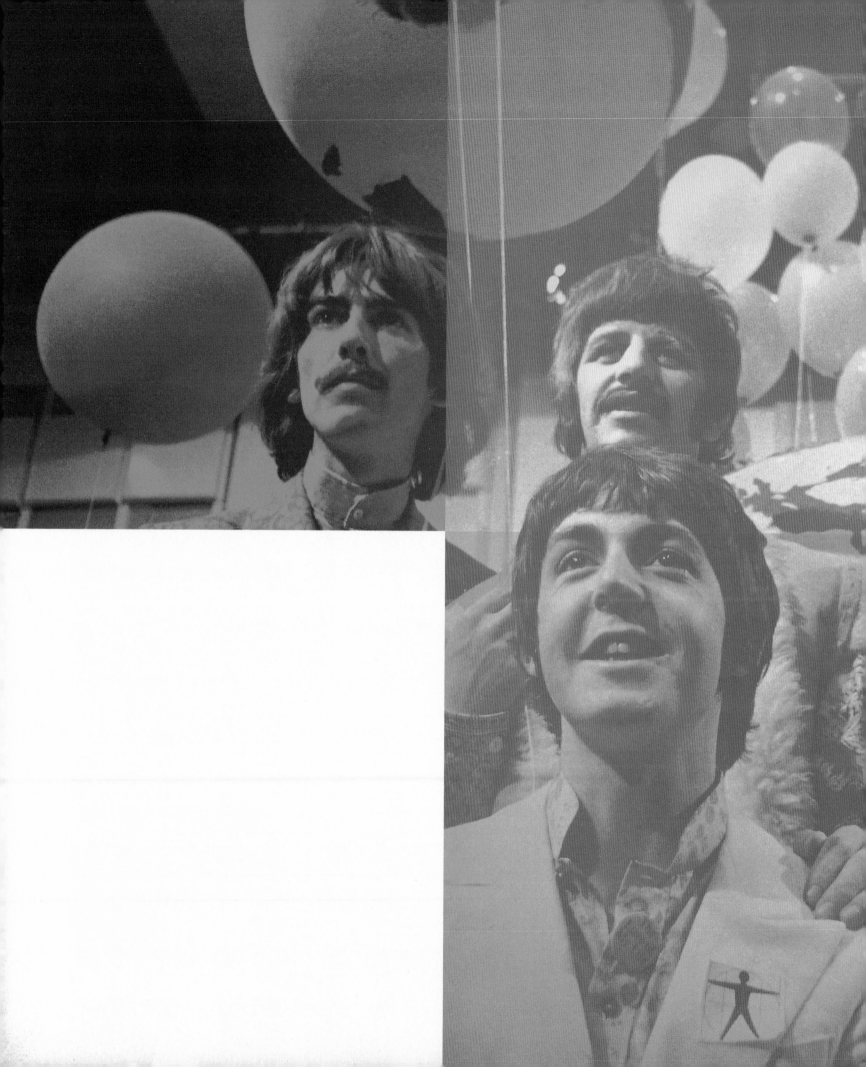

1967

DEFINING
AN
ERA

THE REMAINDER OF 1966 WAS DEVOTED MOSTLY TO RECORDING A SINGLE TRACK. WHILE ON LOCATION WITH RICHARD LESTER, JOHN HAD WRITTEN YET ANOTHER SONG THAT HARKED BACK TO HIS CHILDHOOD. IT WAS NAMED AFTER A SALVATION ARMY CHILDREN'S HOME JUST AROUND THE CORNER FROM AUNT MIMI'S HOUSE – STRAWBERRY FIELD. ORIGINALLY INTENDED TO BE A TRACK FOR AN UNNAMED EIGHTH ALBUM, "STRAWBERRY FIELDS FOREVER" INITIALLY ONLY APPEARED ON A DOUBLE "A"-SIDED SINGLE, BACKED BY PAUL'S OWN PAEAN TO HIS LIVERPOOL HOME, "PENNY LANE".

As the most complex recording The Beatles would ever undertake, "Strawberry Fields Forever" called upon George Martin to bring new heights of ingenuity into his armoury of production talents. The song started out as a simple acoustic ballad, but as the group arrangement evolved, it took on a much "heavier" tone, which appealed to John, who had been inspired by some of the new Californian groups of the times. Over the next month, The Beatles recorded numerous takes of the song featuring a variety of different orchestral instrumentation and sonic treatments.

By December, John had settled on two versions that he especially liked – "Take 7" and "Take 26". He asked Martin if there was any way the two versions could be cut together. The producer explained patiently that this would be highly unlikely as the tuning and tempo would inevitably be slightly different. In a modern-day recording studio with sophisticated pitch- and time-stretching technology such a request would have been quite straightforward, but at that time it would only have been possible by manipulating tape recorders. Martin thought that the effect John was after would be impossible to achieve. Nonetheless, on December 22, 1966, Martin, along with his engineer Geoff Emerick, spent a long evening in the studio experimenting with tape recorders. They found to their amazement that by speeding up "Take 7" and slowing down "Take 26", the tuning and tempo matched. It seemed like a miracle.

The definitive "Strawberry Fields Forever" begins with "Take 7" – the instantly recognizable "flute" introduction, played by Paul on the mellotron, a new keyboard that imitated the sounds of other instruments by playing tape recordings of differently pitched notes – in effect, a precursor to the modern-day digital sampler. "Take 7" plays for just under one minute before cutting seamlessly into "Take 26".

The single was issued on February 17, 1967, backed by Paul's "Penny Lane" – another Beatles classic. Critics were quick to hail both songs. But

over the years "Strawberry Fields Forever" has grown and grown to achieve legendary stature. In the eyes of many, it is the greatest seven inches of vinyl ever produced. When viewed in conjunction with the short promotional film that was shot later in the year – an early video, in effect – the impact remains electrifying. Never has there been a set of images that so concisely evoked an era.

In a final irony to the saga, the single also managed to break a different kind of record for The Beatles. In spite of the lofty pourings of the music literati, "Strawberry Fields Forever"/"Penny Lane" became The Beatles' first single since "Love Me Do" *not* to reach the No. 1 spot – it stalled at No. 2, behind "Please Release Me", a ballad by popular crooner Engelbert Humperdinck.

A STROKE OF GENIUS

The New Year kicked off with The Beatles' studio hibernation still in full swing. In fact, right up until Friday, April 21, they virtually had a free run of Abbey Road's Studio Two. Throughout this time they worked and reworked the same material with meticulous precision, ending up with what is surely the most influential album in the history of popular music – *Sgt. Pepper's Lonely Hearts Club Band*.

So much has been written about this album since it first appeared that, like The Beatles themselves, it's difficult to review the work with any objectivity. Its musical and cultural significance simply shoot off the scale. The album was conclusive proof that the development shown before and after *Revolver* was

Previous spread: Before performing 'All You Need Is Love' as part of the *Our World* satellite production, broadcast on June 25, 1967.

Opposite: All you need is love – The Beatles' universal message.

THE BEATLES // SGT. PEPPER'S LONELY HEARTS CLUB BAND

UK label:
Parlophone PMC/PCS 7027

US label:
Capitol 2653

Producer:
George Martin

Release Date:
June 1, 1967

SIDE 1

Sgt. Pepper's Lonely Hearts Club Band (Lennon/McCartney)
With A Little Help From My Friends (Lennon/McCartney)
Lucy In The Sky With Diamonds (Lennon/McCartney)
Getting Better (Lennon/McCartney)
Fixing A Hole (Lennon/McCartney)
She's Leaving Home (Lennon/McCartney)
Being For The Benefit Of Mr Kite (Lennon/McCartney)

SIDE 2

Within You Without You (Harrison)
When I'm Sixty-Four (Lennon/McCartney)
Lovely Rita (Lennon/McCartney)
Good Morning Good Morning (Lennon/McCartney)
Sgt. Pepper's Lonely Hearts Club Band (Lennon/McCartney)
A Day In The Life (Lennon/McCartney)

no freak occurrence. Once again, it displays a supremely confident group at the peak of their creative powers. It also showed beyond doubt, if ever there was any, that in his usual place – out of the spotlight – Martin had not only mastered the craft of pop production, he was quietly rewriting the user manual with each passing year. In fact, he became so celebrated that, on the release of the album, it began to cause resentment in one quarter of the band. As Paul later said, perhaps overstating his case: "The time we got offended ... one of the reviews said, 'This is George Martin's finest album.' We got shook; I mean, we don't mind him helping us ... it's a great help, but it's not his album, folks, you know."

Sgt. Pepper (as it is inevitably abbreviated) started life as a concept album with a general theme of songs that related The Beatles' childhood memories of Liverpool. The first songs to be recorded for the session had been "Strawberry Fields Forever", "Penny Lane" and Paul's "When I'm Sixty Four". When EMI demanded a new single, The Beatles decided to issue the first pair of tracks. The Liverpool theme then stalled and the idea was abandoned. Still wanting to produce a conceptual work, Paul came up with the idea of creating a mythical band, continuing, "Why don't we make

the whole album as though the Pepper band really existed, as though Sgt. Pepper was doing the record?"

The entire album took a total of five months and 700 hours of studio time to record. It cost a record-breaking £25,000 to produce. The music throughout reveals a complexity never before heard on a pop album: at this point only Brian Wilson and The Beach Boys in America were attempting anything on such an ambitious scale. It was seen as a new benchmark in modern music. Yet in spite of the complex production, it has become something of cliché to be reminded that the album was recorded on a four-track tape machine.

It was perhaps the first pop album where such thought had been put into creating an overall structure. The traditional silence between tracks having been cut down to almost nothing, songs are segued, running into one another. *Sgt Pepper* also brought the four Beatles together in a way

Opposite: John Lennon and Paul McCartney returning to Heathrow Airport from holiday in Greece, July 31, 1967.

Below: During a trip to the West Country for some location work on *The Magical Mystery Tour*, September 12, 1967.

that they never would be again. It was as if they were prepared to put aside any personal agendas and simply do their best. It even promulgated a rare genuine Lennon/McCartney collaboration on "A Day In The Life", the track – recorded on two four-track machines linked together – for which the album would ultimately become so hallowed.

As with their previous effort, *Revolver*, Lennon and McCartney were still pulling in very different directions. John's lyrics, aided by a prodigious consumption of LSD, sprawled down an ever more oblique path. His desire to experiment with sound made huge demands on George Martin, and, as a by-product, helped to create a whole new genre of psychedelic music. In contrast, Paul's work was straightforward and craftsmanlike, although, once again, it is his musicianship that shines through track after track. His natural understanding of harmony also gave an added dimension to his work as a bass player. If anyone can be said to have led the way forward on this instrument, it was Paul McCartney – in the pop field at least.

The overall packaging of the *Sgt. Pepper* album was equally unique. It was certainly one of the first gatefold sleeves, and also the first high-profile pop album to include the songs lyrics printed on the sleeve.

It was Paul who came up with the idea of having a sleeve that depicted photographs of The Beatles alongside their heroes. The idea, however, was met with considerable opposition. EMI hated the idea: to them an album sleeve was not considered to be much more than an advertisement, so anything that obscured their prime selling point – The Beatles, themselves – was viewed as a bad thing. Epstein was equally negative about the concept. The band, though, were adamant.

Artist Peter Blake was brought in to work on the project with The Beatles. All four members of the band selected the figures that they wanted to include, and Wendy Moger, one of Epstein's employees, was given the mammoth task of seeking approval of the living names. Not everyone selected was finally included. Three of John's selections – Jesus Christ, Adolf Hitler and Gandhi – were vetoed on grounds of poor taste. Some things would never change.

Blake and his then-wife Jann Haworth prepared the life-size montage which was then assembled in a photographic studio. The characters were a mixture of cardboard cutouts and figures loaned by Madame Tussauds, London's famous wax museum. The Beatles themselves, as photographed by Michael Cooper, were wearing specially commissioned uniforms, Paul having been talked out of his original plan to have The Beatles dressed as members of the Salvation Army.

Sgt. Pepper was publicly and critically received like no other record. It topped the charts all over the world. On its UK release it went straight to No. 1 and stayed there for six long months. It has since sold more than 32 million copies on vinyl, cassette, CD and, more recently, as a digital download: it remains among the biggest-selling albums of all time.

The critics were, to say the least, fulsome in their praise. To the highest-brows of the high-brow newspapers and magazines this was a genuine work of art. *The Times Literary Supplement* called it "a barometer of our times". In the US, *Newsweek*'s Jack Kroll went further, comparing the band with T. S. Eliot and suggesting that, in his eyes, "A Day in the Life" was The Beatles' equivalent to *The Waste Land*.

Opposite: Paul conducts a 41-piece orchestra during recording sessions for *Sgt. Pepper's Lonely Hearts Club Band*, February 15, 1967.

Next spread: The band celebrate the completion of the new album at a press conference held at the home of Brian Epstein, May 19, 1967.

The Beatles had pulled off a pretty neat trick: they were the darlings of the middle-class media; their peers hung on their every move; they were still loved by their former teenage pop audience; their classic commercial tunes appealed to the young and old alike; and, what's more, the acid-heads and mystics understood what it was all "really" about.

A good indication of the album's cultural significance is the increasingly hysterical media stir that accompanies each new anniversary of its release. The tenth anniversary was greeted with reappraisals by the music press and a package that included a picture-disc of the LP. The twentieth anniversary was inevitably too great an opportunity for the media to miss – myriad television programmes and arts magazines all headed with the opening lyric of the album. The twenty-fifth anniversary, which coincided with the release of a new compact disc version, was surrounded by so much industry hype that the album shot back into the charts for yet another stay. It has since, like the other Beatles albums, been remastered, both in mono and stereo, and, at the end of 2010, launched with much hype as an iTunes digital download.

LOVE AND PEACE

With the fuss surrounding *Sgt. Pepper* already in overdrive, within the space of a month The Beatles were ready to make history all over again. A pivotal moment during the summer of 1967 was the first worldwide satellite television linkup. *Our World* was to be a six-hour live television broadcast with 26 participating nations. The total simultaneous television audience would be 400 million. Each nation nominated its greatest names to take part in this historic attempt at world co-operation: The Beatles were invited to represent Great Britain.

John and Paul decided to pen a new song which would receive its world premier on that occasion. "All You Need Is Love" provided ample proof, were it needed, that The Beatles felt no artistic constraints whatsoever during this period. They composed a ponderous, heavily orchestrated piece of music, the verses of which were played seven beats to the bar – completely unheard of in pop music. That they managed to turn all of this into a catchy, era-defining epic is testament to their supreme talent as songwriters.

On June 25, 1967, the broadcast went ahead as planned, with The Beatles singing over a pre-recorded backing tape. Two weeks later it was released as The Beatles' fifteenth single – and their eighth to go straight to the No. 1 spot. Appropriately, it occupied the top of the charts throughout the "Summer of Love". Irrespective of its merits, "All You Need Is Love" is, for many, perhaps the one song that will be remembered as having defined the era like no other.

THE LOSS OF BRIAN

The Beatles were now mining new depths of creativity. They'd thrown off the shackles of Beatlemania and had developed an influence that was no longer

measurable in terms of units shifted. To those in the middle of the action, 1967's "Summer of Love" felt like a genuine revolution – a new frontier – and The Beatles were at the heart of that change.

The Beatles' new freedom posed a problem for Brian Epstein. In his element organizing the minutiae of The Beatles' working lives over the past five years, and still only in his early thirties, he was beginning to feel like an increasingly unnecessary part of a machine that was now rolling along happily on its own momentum. It was different when he was managing four clueless young lads: if he wanted them to wear new suits they would; if he wanted them to change their set list, they would; if he told them to tour the Far East, they would. But this was 1967, and while The Beatles unquestionably loved and respected him, they now knew where to draw the line. Martin remembered an occasion during the *Sgt. Peppers* sessions that illustrated the way the balance of power had shifted: "When John had finished singing, he [Brian] switched on the studio intercom and said, 'I don't think that sounded quite right, John.' John looked up at him and said in his most cutting voice: 'You stick to your percentages, Brian. We'll look after the music.'"

Other areas of Epstein's life were equally unsettled. Merseybeat was now history, and of the other acts signed to NEMS, only Gerry Marsden (of The Pacemakers) and a former Cavern employee, Cilla Black, were still enjoying high-profile success, and that was veering the way of popular light entertainment – the West End stage or television variety shows.

And Epstein's personal life was as turbulent as ever. He no longer went to great lengths to hide his sexual orientation, but his frequent excursions to pick up young men at London's Piccadilly Underground station posed an increasing risk for such a prominent figure, making him an attractive target for extortionists.

Although he had acted in a sensible, almost fatherly way to The Beatles, Epstein had leapt into the whole 1960s scene with just as much energy as the rest of the band. However, while it provided John and George with new inspiration, for Epstein the haphazard cocktails of pills and alcohol seemed to be consumed increasingly out of unhappiness. At the end of 1966, in a desperate state of depression, he took an overdose of pills. The suicide attempt was not successful. He looked for psychiatric help, and also checked in to a "drying out" clinic. A few months later, in early 1967, he made another unsuccessful bid to take his life.

Throughout this unhappy period, he attempted to immerse himself in other interests, returning to his first love – the theatre. NEMS bought the lease on the Saville Theatre, located in the less fashionable eastern end of

Opposite: Performing 'All Your Need is Love' on *Our World*, broadcast to the world on June 25, 1967.

Above: Brian Epstein, who discovered and managed The Beatles, was found dead at his home on August 27, 1967.

London's Shaftsbury Avenue. He immediately subsidized a programme of highly rated, non-profit-making drama and dance productions. But all this still left him wanting.

During August 1967, Pattie Harrison read an unprepossessing poster announcing that Maharishi Mahesh Yogi was to give a public lecture. Pattie had always accompanied George on his Indian jaunts, and became every bit as infatuated with Asian culture as her husband. Pattie wanted George to persuade the other Beatles to attend the lecture.

On Thursday, April 24, The Beatles joined a small crowd at the luxury Hilton Hotel, in London's Park Lane. Here they found themselves faced by a little old white-haired Indian wearing a robe, describing, in his unusually high-pitched voice, how they would be able to achieve inner peace through meditation. After the lecture, The Beatles sent word that they would like a private meeting, and were immediately invited to join the Maharishi for the bank holiday weekend on a course of indoctrination at University College, Bangor, on the North Wales coast. They asked Epstein if he would join them, but with plans already in place, he reluctantly turned down the offer.

The media somehow got wind of this fast-unravelling story, and were waiting in force to see the entourage – including Pattie Harrison, Jane Asher, Mick Jagger and his girlfriend Marianne Faithfull – leaving Paddington railway station. Cynthia Lennon missed the train – she had been held back by a policeman who thought she was a fan. She made her own way. And so it was that The Beatles found inner peace.

Meanwhile, Epstein left London to spend the weekend with some friends at Kingsley Hill, his country home. However, during the Friday evening he became restless, and announced that he was returning to his house in Belgravia. His Spanish butler Antonio had seen him return to go up to his room, but, by Sunday, he became concerned when Epstein failed to answer his bedroom intercom. He finally contacted Joanne Newfield, Epstein's personal assistant, who, now sadly used to such drama, drove straight over to Belgravia. They called a doctor who advised that the door should be broken down. There they found Brian Epstein's body in bed – he had died from an overdose of Carbitol.

The death of The Beatles' manager stunned the world. By the evening, the band, returning from their weekend with the Maharishi, were met by a huge crowd of television cameras. They had sought the advice of their guru, who had told them that as Epstein's death was a physical matter, it was not really important. The looks on their faces as they fought their way through the massed ranks of the world's media told another story – they were visibly devastated. Perhaps Epstein never quite realized that, despite often finding himself the butt of sometimes cruel humour, the band knew

at heart he was every bit as much a Beatle as they were. As John would later say, "Brian was a beautiful guy."

The coroner confirmed that Epstein had indeed died from an overdose of the Bromide-based sleeping drug Carbitol. However, although his death was registered as "accidental" his sad demise has been the subject of much speculation over the years. While most believe this was no accident, some biographers have speculated that Epstein fell foul of a murder plot related to financial issues in America. Although this may seem far-fetched, barely a year later his lawyer David Jacobs was also found dead – a few weeks after he had requested police protection claiming that he was "in terrible trouble".

ROLL UP FOR THE MYSTERY TOUR

Brian Epstein's death made The Beatles even more resolute about controlling their own affairs. Although the world at large still viewed John as the "leader" of The Beatles, Paul began to assert himself with greater regularity. After a triple triumph of "Strawberry Fields Forever", *Sgt. Pepper* and "All You Need Is Love", The Beatles could be forgiven for thinking that they were invincible. The project they had begun just before their manager's death was to be a television musical, *Magical Mystery Tour*. Their credentials as musicians were well beyond dispute, although they may not have developed in the same way

without the tutelage and studio expertise of George Martin. Yet The Beatles launched into *Magical Mystery Tour* like a bunch of first-year film-school students with an unfeasibly large budget. They wrote, produced, directed, starred in, scored and edited the film. That the outcome was amateurish and over-indulgent should come as no surprise. Perhaps it was impressive enough that there had even been an outcome.

The main problem was the simple logistics of organizing such a project. It was precisely the type of thing at which Epstein had always excelled. The Beatles wanted to hire Shepperton Studios, but hadn't realized that it had to be booked months in advance. This was just one example of four young men – for so long hidden from the tedious front-end activities of their industry – failing to get to grips with such worldly matters as planning.

The filming was a fiasco. Paul's "story" was inspired by the antics of American "Merry Prankster" Ken Kesey, who two years earlier had found some notoriety by taking a coach troupe of assorted oddballs on

Opposite: After being informed of the death of their former mentor and manager Brian Epstein, August 28, 1967.

Below: 'I Am the Walrus': disguised as animals in a scene from *Magical Mystery Tour*, originally aired December 26, 1967.

Magical Mystery Tour Fancy Dress

Thursday 21 December at 7.45pm

Royal Lancaster Hotel Bayswater Road
Entrance to Westbourne Suite
Telephone 262-6787

No admittance without this card

an acid-crawl of California's endless backwoods. The whole escapade was chronicled with great success by Tom Wolfe in his book *The Electric Kool-Aid Acid Test* (1968). Following the unmistakably English psychedelia of *Sgt. Pepper* with its Victorian and Edwardian regalia, the boundlessly parochial Paul anglicized the Ken Kesey experience. Viewing it as if it were an English working-class seaside outing, he populated his tour bus with sideshow freaks and renegades from the musical hall era. Paul's idea was that the bus would travel around and experience the magic of the English countryside.

Following the flimsiest of scripts, The Beatles hired a luxury coach, selected actors from agency directories and set off to make their film. It all sounded so easy – well, it *had* been when Richard Lester did it, anyway. As Neil Aspinall, The Beatles' long-standing personal friend who was employed as a road manager, said of the experience, "What we should have been filming was the chaos we caused." With no itinerary to speak of, the coach would go wherever a Beatle wanted it to, always followed by an army of pressmen keen to discover what was going on. There was mayhem as the coach ambled along tiny country lanes creating traffic jams, and to make matters worse, at the end of the day's filming nobody had thought to book a hotel for the large entourage. The one phrase in the minds if not on the tongues of everyone close to The Beatles was the same – "Epstein wouldn't have let this happen."

When the tour came to an end, The Beatles found themselves with over ten hours of material. They originally thought that they could spend around a week editing the film together. In the end, it took 11 weeks to create a one-hour picture.

Of the musical recording sessions, the end of November saw Paul's "Hello Goodbye" reach No. 1 in the charts, although, these days, The Beatles could no longer be guaranteed of getting there the first week of release. Two weeks later the soundtrack for *Magical Mystery Tour* was issued. A unique format was chosen for the soundtrack – a pair of seven-inch EPs with a gatefold sleeve and a 24-page booklet telling the story of the film through a series of photographs and cartoon strips. A highly attractive and interesting package, it reached No. 2 in the singles charts, being held off the top spot over the Christmas period by "Hello Goodbye".

The critical reaction to the music was generally disappointing. Most agreed that with "I Am The Walrus", John was still pushing back the frontiers of psychedelia, and like his other benchmarks it would influence countless bands in the future. The other tracks, although pleasant enough, were second-rate by the extraordinary standards The Beatles had created for themselves. Perhaps they had just overstretched themselves, or the aftermath of Epstein's death had cast such a long shadow over the whole proceedings.

In America, although Capitol was now contractually obliged to issue US albums in the same form as their UK releases, such a rider did not exist for singles. Consequently, *Magical Mystery Tour* was issued as a full-length album in America, with the songs from the two EPs on side one, and singles from the period making up side two. The additional tracks are "Hello Goodbye", "Strawberry Fields Forever", "Penny Lane", "Baby You're A Rich Man" and "All You Need Is Love" – surely a contender for the greatest single side of an LP ever. When it was released in America, *Magical Mystery Tour* became Capitol's fastest grossing LP to date, doing over $8 million worth of business in the space of three weeks.

If the reception for the music had been disappointing, The Beatles could not have foreseen the hostility with which their film would be received when it was broadcast on Boxing Day 1967. Although filmed in colour – naturally, in line with the psychedelic mood of the day – the BBC chose to show it in black and white. Some 15 million viewers tuned in for what many had hoped would be a visual equivalent to the triumph of *Sgt. Pepper*. Most were disappointed. The following day the British press gave it a unanimous thumbs-down, the critic in the *Daily Express* – a Beatles fan – went as far as to say that in his view there had never been such "blatant rubbish" broadcast on British television.

In retrospect, it's clear that the critics overreacted. While *Magical Mystery Tour* was undeniably no great (or even small) masterpiece, it did have its entertaining moments of "Beatle-ness". In some ways the film has improved with age, no longer under the pressure of such extraordinary expectation. Also, the "pointlessness" at the heart of it is far more in tune with today's mainstream. Paul, who was the driving force behind the project, still defends *Magical Mystery Tour* to this day. Then again, home movies are usually of most interest to the people who made them.

Opposite above: During the filming of *Magical Mystery Tour*, 1967.

Opposite below: *Magical Mystery Tour* party invitation, December 21, 1967.

Below: The Beatles' drumskin, which appeared in the LP cover of *Sgt. Pepper's Lonely Hearts Club Band*.

Top: The tour bus stuck on the bridge near Widecombe, Devon, September 12, 1967.

Left: During the filming of *Magical Mystery Tour*, Plymouth Hoe, September 12, 1967.

Opposite: Paul looking unimpressed during filming, September 14, 1967.

6 8

T H E

R O T

S E T S

I N

1968 WAS TO BE THE BEGINNING OF THE END. FOR THE BEATLES, THE LONG MARRIAGE WAS NOW SHOWING SIGNS OF STRESS. IN SPITE OF PERIODIC EFFORTS TO KEEP THINGS RUNNING SMOOTHLY, 1968 WAS TO SHOW THAT THE BEATLES WERE NOW MUCH LESS A GROUP THAN FOUR INDIVIDUALS INTENT ON DOING THEIR OWN THING. AFTER THE FIASCO OF *MAGICAL MYSTERY TOUR*, THE BAND, IMPERVIOUS TO THE NEED FOR OUTSIDE MANAGEMENT, DECIDED TO PUSH THEIR ENTREPRENEURIAL FLAIR TO THE LIMIT. JOHN AND PAUL RATHER FANCIED THE IDEA OF BEING ALTERNATIVE BUSINESSMEN.

In the middle of 1967, The Beatles had come into contact with Simon Posthuma and Marijka Koger, a pair of young Dutch hippie clothes designers. Collectively they called themselves "The Fool". On arrival in London earlier in the year, after their own Amsterdam enterprise had failed, they found work as theatrical designers. Having been hired for one of Epstein's Saville Theatre productions, they quickly found their way – by virtue of their status as bona fide "beautiful people" – into the epicentre of The Beatles' family. They were soon working almost exclusively for the band, designing the clothes for the *Our World* television spectacle, interior designing George's home, and painting John's psychedelic Rolls-Royce.

In December 1967, The Fool, with a budget of £100,000 from The Beatles, opened up a store. The Apple Boutique – Paul chose the name after a painting by the French artist Magritte – was situated in a four-story house at 94 Baker Street. It would be, according to Paul, "A beautiful place where you could buy beautiful things." John's old school friend Pete Shotton was called down from Liverpool to manage the operation.

The boutique was only the start – The Beatles planned to own an empire where *they* were in control. There would be no stuffy middle-aged "suits" telling them what to do – all the business decisions would be their own. Next in the line was Apple Electronics – one of their more unusual business decisions. John had met a Greek electronics wizard – at least that's what he had claimed – named Alexis Mardas. "Magic Alex", as John renamed him, would create all kinds of pointless electronic gizmos that Lennon found so fascinating. A particular favourite was the "Nothing Box" – a small hand-held device that displayed a series of red lights at random – which John would spend acid-drenched hours staring at, trying to guess which light would come on next. Magic Alex had all manner of wild ideas that the technologically illiterate John found appealing. After criticizing as old-fashioned (much to the annoyance of George Martin) EMI's new eight-track studio at Abbey Road, The Beatles hired him to build Apple Studios. Alex told them that it

would be a 72-track tape machine! What's more, sound dividing screens would be replaced by invisible "fields".

From there The Beatles went Apple crazy. There was Apple Records, Apple Films, Apple Music and Apple Books. The whole operation came under the umbrella Apple Corps Ltd. "It's a pun!" Paul explained helpfully to the press.

A PERIOD OF MEDITATION

With the new business up and running, and a new single "Lady Madonna" ready for release in their absence, February 1968 saw The Beatles embark on a planned three-month period studying meditation under their guru, the Maharishi Mahesh Yogi. The Maharishi's Indian ashram was situated in Rishikesh, overlooking the River Ganges. Despite the primitive lifestyle of the region's inhabitants, the Maharishi lived in the relative luxury of a fenced compound. Along with The Beatles and their partners, came a fine selection of interested celebrities – Mike Love of The Beach Boys, actress Mia Farrow and hippie folk singer Donovan.

The three months of religious tuition, chanting sessions and transcendental meditation, would prove a testing time for a group of people who had become well used to being pampered. Ringo was the first one to crack. Despite having taken a large supply of baked beans with him, he and Maureen made their exit after only ten days and flew back to Blighty – Ringo claimed to have had enough of the spicy vegetarian food. Two months in, Paul and Jane Asher had also had enough. John and George stayed on, but were alarmed at some of the rumours that were beginning to spread. They had already formed the impression that the Maharishi's intended relationship with Mia Farrow

Previous spread: Paul, Jane Asher, Maureen Starr and Ringo, boarding an aeroplane bound for India at London Airport, February 19, 1968.

Opposite: John, Cynthia, George, Pattie Boyd and her sister Jenny leave Heathrow Airport for two months' transcendental meditation at Rishikesh, February 15, 1968.

was perhaps less spiritual than might have been appropriate for such a holy man. When news broke that a young Californian nurse was alleging that the great one had made sexual advances toward her, they too decided that enough was enough.

Returning home, The Beatles faced a barrage of questions from a media keen to make the most of this public humiliation. To their credit, they were as honest as they could be about the situation. "We made a mistake," Paul told them. "We thought there was more to him than there was. He's human. We thought at first that he wasn't." And that was that. No more Maharishi.

Despite this disappointment, the whole experience had generally been a positive one. John in particular used it as a way of overcoming his growing drug dependency, and the removal from their usual surroundings had given them a creative boost. In all, they came back from Rishikesh with a vast array of new material – over 30 new songs.

ENTER YOKO

As The Beatles returned to London, they would have known little about the new figure who was about to burst into their lives. In 1966, John had met a Japanese avant-garde artist named Yoko Ono, who had an exhibition in London. Not only had John been attracted to her, he had also appreciated her work and found conversation with her provocatively inspiring. He had intended to collaborate at some future date, but as yet their plans had come to nothing. In the middle of May 1968, with Cynthia away on holiday, John invited Ono to his Surrey home to work on a series of sound collages. From that day onwards John and Ono became virtually inseparable. The Beatles had seen nothing like it before – no one had ever managed to break their way into the inner sanctum. This posed a major crisis for John. While he still cared for "Cyn", he really thought that Ono – seven years his senior – was his soulmate.

Her influence immediately began to permeate the heart of even The Beatles' most hallowed territory – the studio. Wives and friends had often visited The Beatles while they were recording at Abbey Road, but they would invariably sit in the control room with Martin and his engineer. Everybody knew it was only The Beatles who were allowed into the "live" room. Not any more. Throughout the subsequent recording sessions, John would sit, guitar in hand, just as he had at any time over the past six years, but now he had a constant companion by his side, whispering suggestions into his ear. Yoko Ono was always there.

The sessions for the new album were punctuated by a good deal of bad feeling. Not only was Yoko's presence damaging the already fragile atmosphere of the studio, Paul began to assert his new leadership, often in a heavy-handed way. After criticism about his playing, Ringo, feeling increasingly marginalized, walked out on the band for two weeks. Enthusiastically intending to keep things on course, Paul took over the drumming in his absence. Things became similarly fractious between Paul and George. Only John was oblivious to all of this bad feeling – he had other things to occupy his mind.

Halfway through the recording sessions, on August 26, 1968, a new single was issued. It was momentous for The Beatles as it was to be their debut release on the new Apple label. The song selected was one that Paul

Opposite: The Beatles' spiritual guru – Mahesh Prasad Varma, or the Maharishi Mahesh Yogi – graduated in physics before coaching his students in a meditation technique learnt from his master (and spiritual leader of a monastery near the Tibetan border), which he called Transcendental Meditation, March 1968.

had written while he was visiting Cynthia and Julian Lennon. He says: "I happened to be driving out to see Cynthia. I think it was just after John and she had broken up, and I was quite mates with Julian ... I was going out in my car just vaguely singing this song ... 'Hey Jules ... don't make it bad.' Then I just thought a better name was Jude."

Even while it looked as if they were falling apart, The Beatles could still produce timeless material. "Hey Jude" was an epic lasting over seven minutes. After Paul's simple uplifting song, the famous singalong chant gradually fades out over a four-minute period. A single of such length was bound to cause difficulties for radio stations – some advised The Beatles that this would necessarily reduce playlist potential. They needn't have worried – "Hey Jude" would become The Beatles' biggest-selling single, eventually topping the eight million mark. Within weeks of its release on August 26, it had topped the charts in Britain, America, Canada, Japan, Germany, Holland, Ireland, Belgium, Malaysia, Singapore, New Zealand, Sweden, Norway, and Denmark. It was the biggest-selling single of 1968 and the most performed song for the next three years.

From May until October, The Beatles worked in the studio. In fact, they sometimes worked in several studios at the same time. This was to be the hallmark of their next album. Although the band played together on most of the tracks, it was invariably the composer who would go away and finish it. Only Paul, as self-defined overseer, attended studio sessions on every single day.

Inevitably, this was to produce a very different sounding band. In many ways it was their biggest ever change in direction – although not everyone would see it as a major leap forward. The new album would be a polar opposite to their *Sgt. Pepper* triumph. Everything would be pared down to basics. No more brightly coloured psychedelic sleeves – this one would be plain white. No more big sound production jobs – this one would see songs recorded as simply as possible, many of them using the acoustic guitars on which they had been written while sitting around the ashram in Rishikesh. As for the name of the album? Just *The Beatles*.

The sessions for the *The Beatles* – or *The White Album* as it would be forever known – had yielded well over 30 new songs. That was over two albums' worth of new material that The Beatles wanted to be released in a single package. George Martin was worried. To his ears, although there was material of the highest standard, some of it was also, in his opinion, simply not good enough. He pleaded with the band to pare it down to 14 songs that would fit on a single album. The Beatles remained adamant.

In retrospect, this could perhaps be seen as the one time that Martin got it wrong. For all of *The White Album*'s eccentricities – and it does have its weaker moments – there has surely never been such a magnificent double album package. Miraculous, given the independent spirit in which it was made. But were it not for the tensions and in-fighting in the band – four individuals wanting to have their own way – *The Beatles* may not have ended up at such a feast of creativity. John would later refer to it as their first unselfconscious album.

Unleashed on the world on November 22, 1968, *The Beatles* quickly became the fastest-selling album of all time. It was a major success throughout the world – even reaching No. 7 in the Swedish *singles* chart. *The Beatles* has now sold over 20 million albums, and is one of the ten best-selling albums of all time in America.

Opposite: Scenes of mayhem ensued as The Beatles closed down the Apple Boutique on August 31, 1968, giving away their stock to the public: in barely six months, the store lost over £200,000.

Next spread: Yoko, John and Paul arrive at the opening of the film *Yellow Submarine*, London, July 18, 1968.

THE BEATLES // WHITE ALBUM

UK label:
Apple PCS 7067/8

US label:
Apple 101/2

Producer:
George Martin

Release Date:
November 22, 1968

SIDE 1

Back In The USSR (Lennon/McCartney)
Dear Prudence (Lennon/McCartney)
Glass Onion (Lennon/McCartney)
Ob-La-Di, Ob-La-Da (Lennon/McCartney)
Wild Honey Pie (Lennon/McCartney)
The Continuing Story Of Bungalow Bill (Lennon/McCartney)
While My Guitar Gently Weeps (Harrison)
Happiness Is A Warm Gun (Lennon/McCartney)

SIDE 2

Martha My Dear (Lennon/McCartney)
I'm So Tired (Lennon/McCartney)
Blackbird (Lennon/McCartney)
Piggies (Harrison)
Rocky Raccoon (Lennon/McCartney)
Don't Pass Me By (Starkey)
Why Don't We Do It In The Road? (Lennon/McCartney)
I Will (Lennon/McCartney)
Julia (Lennon/McCartney)

SIDE 3

Birthday (Lennon/McCartney)
Yer Blues (Lennon/McCartney)
Mother Nature's Son (Lennon/McCartney)
Everybody's Got Something To Hide Except Me and My Monkey (Lennon/McCartney)
Sexy Sadie (Lennon/McCartney)
Helter Skelter (Lennon/McCartney)
Long Long Long (Harrison)

SIDE 4

Revolution 1 (Lennon/McCartney)
Honey Pie (Lennon/McCartney)
Savoy Truffle (Harrison)
Cry Baby Cry (Lennon/McCartney)
Revolution 9 (Lennon/McCartney)
Good Night (Lennon/McCartney)

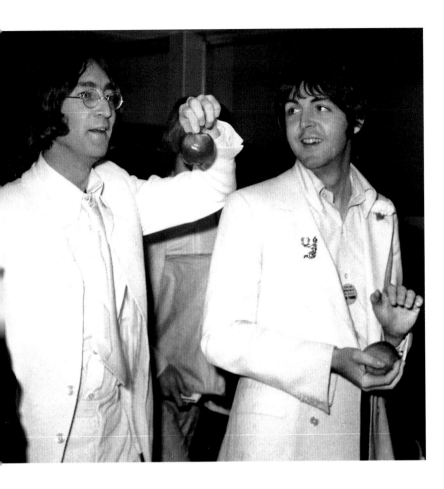

Some of the critics were cautiously positive, feeling slightly let down after *Sgt. Pepper*. Others, like the *Observer's* music critic Tony Palmer, went into overdrive, claiming *The Beatles* would "see the last vestiges of cultural snobbery and bourgeois prejudice swept away in a deluge of joyful music making, which only the ignorant will not hear and only the deaf will not acknowledge." More than 40 years later, the album is still lauded, appearing in tenth position on *Rolling Stone Magazine's* 2003 list of the 500 Greatest Albums Ever Made.

THE ROTTEN APPLE

Without the guiding hand of manager Epstein, it was becoming increasingly difficult to pinpoint exactly what was going on in The Beatles' camp. Apple Corps had now taken a leap into the public domain as John and Paul proudly announced the birth of the Apple Foundation for the Arts. The aims would be, as Paul put it, "A kind of Western Communism ... we're in a happy position of not needing any more money so for the first time the bosses are not in it for the profit. If you come to me and say 'I've had such and such a dream', I'll say to you, 'Go away and do it.'"

The Beatles were planning to be the Medicis of the hippie era – almost. Predictably, the Foundation was immediately inundated with every conceivable type of proposal that might have been considered in the realm of the arts: demo tapes, poems, novels, film treatments – every invention imaginable.

With Apple Corps ballooning by the day, the offices above the Baker Street boutique were now hopelessly inadequate. Aspinall was given the task of finding a new address, and within days The Beatles took over the lease of a five-storey Georgian building in the heart of London's Mayfair. Number three Savile Row was about to become the headquarters for one of the most absurdly unsuccessful business ventures of the era.

While Apple was sprawling out of control before their very eyes, one part of the empire was immediately successful. With music being, after all, something The Beatles knew a bit about, it was not so surprising that the Apple record label would be a big success. Their very first signing was an American singer-songwriter named James Taylor, who despite failing to score a hit for the label, would eventually become one of the most successful artists of the early 1970s. Like Taylor, few of the early signings achieved major commercial success – Welsh singer Mary Hopkin, English band Badfinger and The Radha Krishna Temple being the exceptions. Apple was, however, responsible for many other fine releases – artists such as Jackie Lomax, Trash, The Hot Chocolate Band (later to find great success simply as Hot Chocolate), Billy Preston, The Modern Jazz Quartet, Doris Troy and English classical composer John Tavener.

1968 also saw the conclusion of a somewhat tiresome project that had been hanging around for nearly two years – a Beatles animated film. The band hated the idea, and deliberately had very little involvement, agreeing to supply four new songs and a live action sequence to the ending. The results, however, were surprising. In fact, while the fun-loving Fab Four who appear in *Yellow Submarine* (1968) were by now virtually unrecognizable, the film was something of a triumph of cinema animation. The brightly coloured psychedelic images captured the era with perfection. Even the script – written by, among others, a Yale English professor named Erich Segal (who would write the best-selling classic *Love Story* two years later) – amalgamating stories and characters from the *Revolver* and *Sgt. Pepper* albums was entertaining and, in its own way, quite coherent.

The Beatles attended the premiere of the movie. John took the opportunity to do a premiere of his own – his first public appearance with Yoko. *Yellow Submarine* was greeted ecstatically by film and animation critics. Although The Beatles had little to do with the film's creation, as the *Daily Telegraph* reported, "The Beatles' spirit is here." Alexander Walker of the *Evening Standard* described it as "The key film of The Beatles' era ... a trip through contemporary mythology."

While the film was one of the year's biggest hits in America, it was pretty much killed off at birth in the UK, with distributor Rank bizarrely choosing not to give it a full release. Although the movie was widely acclaimed, The Beatles themselves received few plaudits for their four new songs, which really did seem to have been knocked out in the studio to fulfill a contractual obligation. George's "Only a Northern Song" is a humourless dig at his own publishing contract which meant that, as principle shareholders in Northern Songs, John and Paul made more publishing money on George's songs than he did. His other effort "It's All Too Much" is about his LSD experiences. Paul's "All Together Now" is a simple children's nursery rhyme. John's "Hey Bulldog" was recorded and mixed in the space of one afternoon – an illustration, perhaps, of the way the Fab Four were each beginning to feel about life as a Beatle.

Above: John and Paul at London Airport after a trip to America to promote their new company Apple Corps, 16 May, 1968.

Opposite: The Beatles hold a submarine during their announcement to make the animated film *Yellow Submarine* later released in 1968.

Next spread: Ringo and George with two Blue Meanies, characters who appear in their film *Yellow Submarine*, July 8, 1968.

69

ONE

LAST

SHOT

AS 1968 CAME TO A CLOSE, APPLE CORPS WAS, IF NOT YET COMPLETELY ROTTEN, CERTAINLY SHOWING SIGNS OF HAVING GONE OFF. APPLE FILMS AND APPLE BOOKS HAD YET TO RELEASE A SINGLE PRODUCT. APPLE ELECTRONICS, IN SPITE OF THE HEAVY SUBSIDY, LOOKED INCAPABLE OF PRODUCING A VIABLE PRODUCT. THE APPLE FOUNDATION FOR THE ARTS HAD STALLED – THERE WERE SIMPLY NOT THE RESOURCES TO EVEN LOOK AT THE APPLICATIONS, LET ALONE JUDGE THEIR WORTH. THE APPLE BOUTIQUE WAS A DISASTER FROM DAY ONE.

So much so that on moving to Savile Row, The Beatles themselves took the decision to close it down – as Paul told the press, "The Beatles are tired of being shopkeepers."

The termination process was a simple one. One evening, The Beatles and their families visited the shop and helped themselves to anything they fancied. The following day they told the world it could do the same. Hundreds of eager shoppers, held in check by a dozen policemen, fought their way through the doors and made off with anything they could lay their hands on.

The Beatles were selling as well as ever, but their business affairs were now well and truly out of control. The solution to this problem would ultimately result in their bitterest disagreement. Seen by the media as having a license to print money, there would clearly be no shortage of offers to take over from where Epstein had left off. An early contender in 1967 had been Australian impresario Robert Stigwood, who was a partner in NEMS. Stigwood went on to huge success managing the Bee Gees, and producing *Grease* and *Saturday Night Fever* – two of the biggest movies of the late 1970s. His interest in The Beatles didn't end there. In 1978, he produced a musical version of *Sgt. Pepper's Lonely Hearts Club Band* starring the Bee Gees with 1977's flavour-of-the-moment Peter Frampton taking the role of Billy Shears. The film was universally slated and bombed spectacularly at the box office. However, Stigwood astutely realized that a potentially huge market lay in soundtrack albums – *Saturday Night Fever* remains one of the biggest-selling albums of all time.

The soundtrack to *Sgt. Pepper* featured covers of most of the songs on the original album, plus 18 other Beatle hits, performed by a selection of stars of the day. Although the album sold in Beatle-like quantities, the briefest of listens would show that while they were the most covered band in pop history, it was nigh on impossible to improve on the originals – although funksters Earth Wind & Fire certainly had a bold stab with their dynamic take on "Got To Get You Into My Life".

It was Allen Klein, America's foremost showbiz lawyer, who put a halt to Apple's decay. In doing so he would also play a significant role in the band's eventual demise. The Beatles had been aware of Klein as far back as 1966, when

Mick Jagger, by whom Klein had been employed as a business advisor, told them that, although they were selling far more records than the Rolling Stones, they were making a lot less money. Although Paul had initially suggested that Epstein should speak to Klein, nothing happened. When The Beatles formed Apple, Klein approached them, but at that time they were more interested in doing things for themselves and didn't even reply to his communications. Now, though, with everything in such a mess, John took the initiative and arranged a meeting. Apparently impressed by the fact that he knew John's songs, and that he wasn't a "suit" like all the other businessmen, John convinced George and Ringo that he should be their own representative.

Matters were more difficult for Paul. The previous year, with his relationship with Asher becoming increasingly problematic, he started to get to know a New York photographer called Linda Eastman. Their relationship flourished quickly and they were soon discussing marriage. Paul was now faced with a tricky family dilemma: Linda's father and brother were partners in the New York law firm Eastman & Eastman, and Paul now wanted them to represent The Beatles. An uneasy alliance was created that allowed everybody's involvement, although Klein was effectively in charge. This would not provide the unified management that The Beatles had been looking for – at every possible future crossroads the interests of Paul and the others were seen to be at odds. It would ultimately provide the spark for their separation.

GET BACK TO BASICS

Paul was still the motivating force behind the band. A born musician, he felt a strong need to perform in front of an audience. His colleagues didn't quite

Previous spread: On the roof of the Apple offices for The Beatles' last ever public performance, January 30, 1969.

Opposite: Paul and Linda McCartney at the premiere of *Isadora*, London, March 5, 1969.

see it in the same way. Concerned by the apathy that seemed to be spreading throughout the band, Paul thought that if they had a goal to work toward – maybe a one-off filmed concert performance – it might bring some life and enthusiasm into The Beatles. A number of ideas were thrown about. Some were reasonably practical, such as a series of shows at The Roundhouse in London's Chalk Farm. Others were more surreal – a live broadcast from a stage in the middle of the Sahara Desert. While Paul's impetus hardly brought about the overwhelmingly enthusiastic response he'd been looking for, the others reluctantly agreed. TV producer Denis O'Dell, who was hired to organize the event, also suggested that rehearsals for the show be recorded for an alternative television documentary.

The taped rehearsals, at Twickenham Film Studios, began on January 15. The tensions were palpable from the start. Once again, to the annoyance of the others, Yoko never seemed to be more than a few feet away from John. The main problem, though, was that Paul was the only Beatle who really wanted to be there. His annoyance at the antipathy surrounding him spilled over into arguments about playing. The other three, for their part, were clearly beginning to tire of his over-assertiveness. George, in particular, became irritated that Paul was telling him exactly how he wanted things played – something that had never really happened previously in The Beatles. In one incident, filmed for the world to see, an exasperated George, having been told how to play his instrument once too often, just snaps back at Paul, "Look, just tell me how you want me play it and I'll play it, OK?" Shortly afterwards, George quietly walked out and spent the best part of the next week in Liverpool with his parents. Seemingly oblivious to his absence, the filming and rehearsals went on without him. He eventually returned with as little ado as his departure.

The recording of the new album – still untitled, but referred to as *Get Back* – had been scheduled to take place in Magic Alex's new Apple Studios in the basement of Savile Row. At the end of January, The Beatles turned up to start recording only to find complete chaos. Far from the 72-track studio their in-house boffin had promised, the scene was more reminiscent of a home-built electronics laboratory with dozens of tiny loudspeakers placed all around the studio. Despite the dubious-looking surroundings. they decided to try some test recordings, but these only proved their worst fears. Magic Alex might have possessed an innovative mind, but he was equally incapable of producing anything usable. The next two days were spent undoing his handiwork and hiring mixing consoles from Abbey Road.

The recording went more smoothly than one would have expected, judging by the rehearsals. As the idea for *Get Back* was, indeed, for a return to a more spontaneous live type of recording, The Beatles brought in an extra musician – George's friend Billy Preston, an outstanding keyboard player. The presence of an outsider seemed to relax the tensions that had made the Twickenham experience so unpleasant. As Paul said, "You know what it's like when you have company ... you try and be on your best behaviour."

UP ON THE ROOF

Meanwhile, plans were being changed behind the scenes. *The Beatles* had used up the back-catalogue of the band's unrecorded material, and the new songs were taking their time to develop. The budget for filming the live performance couldn't possibly stretch through the recording of an entire album – that could last up to six months. An alternative schedule was hastily hatched. It was decided that on Thursday, January 30, The Beatles would perform an unannounced concert on the roof of their Savile Row headquarters. This would be the live performance that would be filmed.

At lunchtime on the great day, The Beatles took to the impromptu stage at the top of the building surrounded by family, friends and film crews. They struck up the opening chords of "Get Back". Within minutes, local office workers began to investigate the noise. Gradually, the narrow roads around Mayfair became more and more congested, until the police inevitably came to investigate the commotion. Finally, after 42 minutes of playing, and distracted by the number of police officers who were by now trying to get them to stop the music, the show came to an end with a second version of "Get Back". After a final crash of the cymbals, with the guitar chords fading, Paul shouts out, "Thanks Mo!" to Ringo's wife who is applauding wildly. John then quips, "I'd like to say thank you on behalf of the group and ourselves and I hope we pass the audition." And that was The Beatles' final public performance.

With the filming over, The Beatles spent the next day duplicating their roof-top performance in the studio for the *Get Back* album. It all seemed very straightforward – they just wanted to record a set of songs as they had done

Opposite: George Harrison and his wife
Pattie Boyd on their way to Nice, France,
September 1969.

THE BEATLES // ABBEY ROAD

UK label:
Apple PCS 7088

US label:
Apple 383

Producer:
George Martin

Release Date:
September 26, 1969

SIDE 1

Come Together (Lennon/McCartney)
Something (Harrison)
Maxwell's Silver Hammer (Lennon/McCartney)
Oh Darling (Lennon/McCartney)
Octopus's Garden (Starkey)
I Want You (She's So Heavy) (Lennon/McCartney)

SIDE 2

Here Comes The Sun (Harrison)
Because (Lennon/McCartney)
You Never Give Me Your Money (Lennon/McCartney)
Sun King (Lennon/McCartney)
Mean Mr Mustard (Lennon/McCartney)
Polythene Pam (Lennon/McCartney)
She Came In Through The Bathroom Window (Lennon/McCartney)
Golden Slumbers (Lennon/McCartney)
Carry That Weight (Lennon/McCartney)
The End (Lennon/McCartney)

on that first day at Abbey Road with George Martin. That it could have been so simple...

After spending much of February trying to finish off the album, their enthusiasm – even Paul's – began to dwindle. The Beatles decided to bring in producer Glyn Johns. They handed over the pile of master tapes to him and invited him to finish it. The Beatles had reached rock bottom – they had recorded an album that they couldn't be bothered to finish. As John said: "We didn't want to know about it anymore, so we just left it ... and said 'Here, mix it.' None of us could be bothered going in. Nobody called anybody about it, and the tapes were left there. Glyn Johns did it. We got an acetate in the mail."

The results were considerably worse than they had expected. 29 hours of music had been mixed down to a single album – they had wanted it to sound raw, but not as raw as this. They debated releasing it in that state. John was particularly keen: "I didn't care. I thought it was good to let it out and show people what had happened to us...we don't play together anymore, you know, leave us alone."

They decided to sit on the project for the moment. The only tangible fruits of those sessions in 1969 were a pair of singles. Paul's "Get Back" was released in April, followed by John's "The Ballad of John and Yoko", on which John plays guitars and Paul drums and piano. Despite everything, the public were clearly still interested in The Beatles – both singles were, again, worldwide No. 1 hits.

THE LAST TRY

The coming months saw The Beatles embroiled in legal wranglings of the Klein-Eastman variety. They also started to spend more time working on their own projects. John and Yoko were making something of a name for themselves as fledgling peace protesters and continued the experimental sound collages like "Revolution 9", which so many people either hated or laughed at. Ringo was now pursuing what looked like a plausible acting career, starring in *The Magic Christian* (1969). George was actively engaged in production work and Paul simply busied himself writing songs and learning how to record his own music.

Then, in June 1969, Paul contacted George Martin with an unexpected request – that The Beatles wanted to record an album with him, just as they had done with *Revolver* and *Sgt. Pepper*. Martin, although sceptical, agreed to one more try, and Abbey Road was block-booked for the first three weeks of July. Once again, everyone was on their best behaviour, putting their differences behind them and concentrating on the only thing they had left in common – music.

The album was to be called *Abbey Road* – apt as it was the home of nearly all of their classic recordings. From its release date at the end of August, the album was seized on by fans as undeniable proof that The Beatles were genuinely "together" again. While *The Beatles* had broken records – it was the fastest-ever selling album at the time of its release – *Abbey Road* sold in even greater quantities. It went to No. 1 in the UK, not budging for the next five months.

Released two months later in the US, it was similarly successful – in fact, at that time, *Sgt. Pepper*, *Magical Mystery Tour* and *The Beatles* still held places in the Top 100 charts. World sales of *Abbey Road* are now well over the 20 million mark, placing it among the 50 biggest-selling albums of all time.

The sleeve, once again eschewing flashy design conventions of the period, was simplicity itself: a photograph of the four Beatles on a zebra crossing outside Abbey Road Studios. The reverse side shows Abbey Road's London street sign. This sleeve made Abbey Road the most famous recording studio in the world. Every year, thousands of tourists from across the globe still visit the studio as if it were a religious shrine. The new street signs disappear almost the moment they are put up. Graffiti on the walls outside the studio's car park are a constant reminder that as far as icons of popular culture go, only Elvis Presley and Michael Jackson come anywhere near The Beatles.

The critics were also now firmly back on their side – the material on *Abbey Road* clearly showed a new maturity. On show for the first time were The Beatles as musicians. George's delicate solo playing showed that years of hanging out with Eric Clapton had done him no harm. Even Ringo, for years the "unmusical" one, was playing with greater confidence than ever – a few minutes from the end of the album he even takes a brief drum solo. Paul, in the meantime, had become a versatile multi-instrumentalist and skilful arranger.

If *Abbey Road* was to give their public hope for the future, The Beatles – John in particular – always knew that it would be their last album. If that was to be the case, *Abbey Road* was a pretty special way to go out. Perhaps the

revelation of the album was that two of its most beautiful and striking songs – "Something" and "Here Comes The Sun" – were both written by George. For many it was the second side of the album, with its short segued tracks creating the effect of a mini-opera, that captured the imagination. *Abbey Road* ends with the vignette "The End" in which Paul sings, "And in the end the love you take is equal to the love you make." And with that The Beatles, and the 1960s – the decade over which they presided – came to an end.

END OF STORY

As far as three of The Beatles were concerned, that was pretty much that. Paul still wanted to keep things going, though. On one occasion, when Paul again tried to push them into playing live, John told the band that he'd had enough. He wanted out. Ringo and George had also walked out – if temporarily – in the recent past. The Beatles left things to simmer.

Previous spread: John Lennon and his wife of a week Yoko Ono receive the press during their Bed-in for Peace in the Hilton Hotel, Amsterdam, March 25, 1969.

Opposite: Allan Klein representing John in negotiations over control of shares in The Beatles' Northern Songs company.

Above: The iconic Abbey Road sign.

Meanwhile, Klein's emergence on the scene had been a dramatic one. He arrived to find Apple Corps in a worse state than he could have imagined. Number three Savile Row already appeared to be a serious mess, but everywhere Klein looked he found an army of paid hangers-on who produced little of any value. Klein scorched his way through Apple Corps, instantly writing off whole departments. Within months he had pared down the organization to the barest of essentials.

Klein had also found the band's contractual affairs in a muddle. The Beatles had mistakenly thought that *Yellow Submarine* constituted the third and final film of their contract with United Artists. They were wrong. Instead of issuing the *Get Back* project as a TV show, Klein decided they had enough material to turn it into a feature-length film that could be sold to United Artists.

Klein's next move was to renegotiate their record deals. This was to be a problem because by now John was insistent that he was leaving the band. Klein asked him to keep silent until he had completed his negotiations. John agreed, although speculation began to increase again in the music press.

The Beatles continued to have very little to do with the *Get Back* project – now retitled *Let It Be* after one of Paul's new songs. But there was one thing on which everyone agreed: no matter how little they cared about the accompanying album, in its current state it was simply not up to scratch. With The Beatles' consent, Alan Klein handed the tapes over to star American producer Phil Spector. In the early 1960s, Spector had found fame with his heavily orchestrated "Wall of Sound" productions that graced hits by, among others, The Ronettes, The Righteous Brothers and Ike and Tina Turner.

The finished version of *Let It Be* is, in many ways, The Beatles' strangest album. Some of the tracks Spector left in a raw, almost unfinished state, even leaving snippets of dialogue – mostly John's sarcastic quips. But the rest of the album had been very heavily doctored, with the addition of orchestras, choirs and brass sections. The Beatles would be in for a surprise.

THE FINAL CURTAIN

While John, George and Ringo were largely ambivalent, Paul was mortified with the finished album, especially as it was his songs that had received most of Spector's attention. He wrote to Klein insisting the original versions of his tracks be reinstated but received no response. In March 1970, he contacted John to tell him that he now intended to leave the group. So, while John had informed the band of his decision six months earlier, it was Paul who, on April 17, sent out a press release accompanying his debut album *McCartney* announcing "his" decision. The Beatles were officially dead.

May 20 saw the film premiere of *Let It Be*. Although Asher and Cynthia Lennon were among the celebrities in attendance, there wasn't a single Beatle. Perhaps it was just too much for any of them to take. John said: "It was hell making the film ... the most miserable session on earth."

The film made the tensions that had been growing for the past three years abundantly clear. It is a fascinating exercise in group dynamics. Everyone looks miserable except Paul, who enthusiastically chivvies the whole facade along. He chatters away endlessly, even though it's quite clear that most of the time nobody is paying attention to a word he's saying.

The final sequence of events turned *Let It Be* into something of a postscript to the story. The album indicates an abundance of apathy. And the film? It simply shows the sad spectacle of four adults who have grown too far apart to be reconciled.

Opposite: A letter from John, George and Ringo, dated 18 April 1969 to Lee Eastman showing evidence of one of the major catalysts behind the disbanding of The Beatles.

Next spread: George Harrison, John Lennon, Paul McCartney and Ringo Starr in 1969.

THE BEATLES // LET IT BE

UK label:
Apple PCS 7096

US label:
Apple 34001

Producer:
George Martin, Glyn Johns, Phil Spector

Release Date:
May 8, 1970

SIDE 1

Two Of Us (Lennon/McCartney)
Dig A Pony (Lennon/McCartney)
Across The Universe (Lennon/McCartney)
I Me Mine (Harrison)
Dig It (Lennon/McCartney/Starkey/Harrison)
Let It Be (Lennon/McCartney)
Maggie May (traditional)

SIDE 2

I've Got A Feeling (Lennon/McCartney)
One After 909 (Lennon/McCartney)
The Long And Winding Road (Lennon/McCartney)
For You Blue (Harrison)
Get Back (Lennon/McCartney)

Eastman and Eastman
39 West 54th Street
New York
New York 10019   18th April 1969

Attention Lee Eastman, Esq.

Dear Mr. Eastman,

    This is to inform you of the fact that you are not
authorized to act or to hold yourself out as the attourney
or legal representative of "The Beatles" or of any of the
companies which the Beatles own or control.

    We recognize that you are authorized to act for
Paul McCartney, personally, and in this regard we will
instruct our representatives to give you the fullest co-
operation.

    We would appreciate your forwarding to

        ABKCO Industries Inc.
        1700 Broadway
        New York
        N.Y.

all documents, correspondence and files which you hold
in your possession relating to the affairs of the Beatles,
or any of the companies which the Beatles own or control.

                    Very truly yours,

                    John Lennon

                    Richard Starkey

                    George Harrison

1970+

WITHOUT THE BEATLES

BY THE TIME PAUL MADE HIS ANNOUNCEMENT THAT THE BEATLES REALLY WERE NO MORE, FEW WERE COMPLETELY SURPRISED. JOHN, PAUL, GEORGE AND RINGO HAD ALREADY BEGUN SOLO CAREERS. IT WAS INEVITABLE THAT A BAND SO UNIVERSALLY SUCCESSFUL, BOTH WITH CRITICS AND AUDIENCES, WOULD SPAWN SOLO CAREERS. AS TWO GIANTS OF POPULAR MUSIC, IT WAS READILY ASSUMED THAT LENNON AND MCCARTNEY WOULD GO ON TO GREATER THINGS – EVEN IF JOHN SEEMED TO BE, FOR THE TIME BEING AT LEAST, UNDER THE CREATIVE SPELL OF YOKO, WHOM HE HAD NOW MARRIED.

Paul, on the other hand, as a master of what John would uncharitably call "Grandma music", seemed destined for a long and distinguished musical career.

Things were less clear for George and Ringo. Although his contributions to the final Beatle albums were of an extremely high standard, less was perhaps expected of George. Still firmly into his Indian religion and culture, he spent more and more time in the company of virtuoso musicians like Clapton.

Ringo, it was supposed, might attempt a few recordings, but a switch to the world of cinema looked to be perhaps more likely: his performances in the two Beatle films had shown a fledgling talent with great potential.

However, one thing was guaranteed. For the foreseeable future, anything that any of The Beatles were involved with would be reported with extreme interest by a media always ready to hold the front page with the two magic words – "BEATLES REFORM". Patiently, they would have to wait...and wait... and wait. And so they did – until the evening of December 8, 1980.

JOHN LENNON – WORKING-CLASS HERO

In 1968, John Lennon had finally got together with Japanese avant-garde artist Yoko Ono. Although Lennon and McCartney had not worked closely together in recent years, Yoko Ono effectively took over the role of John's creative partner. This initially manifested itself in some rather strange experiments, not least of which were John's earliest solo efforts.

The first collaboration was *Unfinished Music No. 1 – Two Virgins*, released in 1968. A series of sound collages – in much the same vein as "Revolution 9" on *The Beatles* – the music itself created little stir. Had they bothered to listen, few of the band's long-standing pop fans would have even considered it to be music in any conventional sense. Controversy, however, surrounded the sleeve, which featured John and Yoko in a full-frontal nude photograph. Eventually, the album was only made available placed in a brown paper bag. Surprisingly, given the popularity of The Beatles, if not the uncompromising music on offer, the album only sold around 5,000 copies and was soon deleted. The following

year, the duo ploughed a similar furrow with similar success, on *Unfinished Music No. 2 – Life With The Lions*, one side of which was recorded on a cassette tape during Yoko's failed pregnancy at Queen Charlotte Hospital. Again, John's bold artistic statement failed to capture a large audience.

In 1969, with the future of The Beatles still unclear, John and Yoko formed the Plastic Ono Band. At this time, they were active propagandists for peace, frequently pulling highly publicized stunts. One such effort was a series of what they termed "bed-ins", one of which took place at the Queen Elizabeth Hotel in Montreal, Canada. For ten days the Lennons' suite became the centre of all manner of media activity. They enjoyed visits from luminary supporters like Dr Timothy Leary, and TV crews from all over the world. It was also the location they chose to record their first single – an anthem for their peace protest, "Give Peace A Chance". That it was crudely recorded and roughly performed was beside the point. John was turning the tables on a media that had for so long fed on The Beatles. He was getting his own back. The single was an immediate success, and has since proved to be the definitive peace anthem throughout the world.

In 1970, John sought to put together a "real" band for future recordings. The most consistent players were Clapton on guitar, Voormann on bass, and Ringo on drums. Controversial singles like "Cold Turkey", a song that documented the agony of John's heroin withdrawal (and that Paul had refused to record with The Beatles) and "Instant Karma" were big hits and boosted his anti-establishment standing.

With The Beatles now firmly in the past, the end of 1970 saw a shift in emphasis in John's music. The messages were still there, but now they

Previous spread: John Lennon and Yoko Ono in Jutland, Denmark where they were living in meditation, January 22, 1970.

Opposite: John and Yoko at the screening of 'The Rape', which Lennon produced for the Golden Rose of Montreux festival, April 27, 1969.

were less often enveloped in chants and sloganeering. After reading *The Primal Scream* (1976), by psychiatrist Dr Arthur Janov, John underwent an intense three-week session of therapy, under the direction of Janov himself. The underlying principles of Primal Scream therapy are that all neuroses are the result of lack of parental love during early childhood. Janov encouraged his patients to exorcise those ghosts by screaming at the absent parents. The impact of his influence can be felt clearly on *John Lennon/The Plastic Ono Band*. Songs such as "Mother", "Isolation", "Look At Me", and "My Mummy's Dead" (recorded by John alone on a portable cassette recorder) dealt with his troubled childhood in a highly confessional manner. To mainstream Beatle fans it looked as if John was at least returning to something they could understand – "real" songs. Many now regard the album as his finest solo work.

1971 was one of John's most commercially successful years. He installed an eight-track recording studio at his home in Tittenhurst Park and it was here that, along with Phil Spector, he produced *Imagine*, his most successful album. A gentler, more commercial sound, combined with more coherent lyrics, *Imagine* found immediate favour with fans of The Beatles. Not only did it feature the haunting melody of the title track – one of the most famous pop songs of all time – it also contains bitter attacks on Paul McCartney in the form of "How Do You Sleep?", and to a lesser extent, "Crippled Inside". *Imagine* topped the charts on both sides of the Atlantic.

By this time, John had for several years been refused entry to America. Ostensibly the result of a drug conviction in 1968, it was now commonly conceded that his anti-capitalist, anti-authoritarian, anti-Vietnam war stance had made him an "undesirable" to the Federal Authorities. In September 1971, when he was finally given permission to enter the US, John and Yoko flew from Heathrow Airport to New York. Over the coming years, he would face many a long battle with the US Immigration Authorities, firstly to prevent his deportation, and secondly to acquire the Green Card that would allow him permanent residency in America. This was finally granted to him in 1976. John never returned to the UK.

The albums that followed *Imagine* – *Mind Games* and *Walls And Bridges* – charted familiar territory, and while his work remained popular, his revolutionary standing began to dwindle. This period also saw the beginning of one of the most turbulent times in his life. For most of the mid-1970s, he was frequently estranged from Yoko, and became heavily involved in the excesses of the celebrity alcohol and drug scene.

By the end of the decade, John seemed to have found a happier lifestyle. Settled once more with Yoko, he began to find simple pleasure in lounging around his luxury apartment at The Dakota Building, overlooking New York's Central Park. He now devoted most of his attention to bringing up their son Sean. With this renewed domestic harmony came a fresh surge of creativity. In 1980 he began work on his first album of new material in six years.

Double Fantasy was released in November 1980. While it won few critical ovations, it was nonetheless well received and, along with an accompanying single "(Just Like) Starting Over", it quickly entered the charts in America and throughout most of Europe. Some saw it as a sign that one of the great creative minds in popular music was back, and ready to tackle a new decade.

Of course, this was not to be. On December 8, 1980, while returning late from a recording session at The Hit Factory, John and Yoko were about to enter the courtyard of The Dakota Building when a voice called out his name. As John turned, a hail of revolver shots rang out and he fell to the ground. He was rushed to Roosevelt Hospital, but pronounced dead on arrival. The assassin had been a disturbed Beatles fanatic named Mark David Chapman.

John Lennon's death stunned the world. He was so much more than merely the founder of the most important pop group in history. While unquestionably capable of acts of cruelty and selfishness, John had publicly stood out for the most positive aspects of humanity. He preached the true spirit of the 1960s – peace, love and understanding – as vociferously, even belligerently, as anyone. The world may have moved on, and some of those ideals may now seem rather naïve, but as philosophies go, there are a whole lot worse that we could embrace.

PAUL MCCARTNEY – GOING FOR IT

There was never any real doubt that Paul McCartney would enjoy some sort of solo success. Even though with each passing year, it was John's contributions to The Beatles that were becoming revered as "old masters", Paul's music had grown to develop the more conventionally commercial edge.

Released in April 1970, *McCartney* was a culmination of Paul's development as a musician over the previous five years. The other Beatles had kicked off

Opposite: John Lennon backstage at BBC TV's *Top Of The Pops* in London, February 11, 1970.

Below: Linda and Paul McCartney on their farm near the fishing town of Campbeltown, January 5, 1970.

their post-Fab careers with celebrity-filled bands but, with the exception of the odd vocal contribution from his wife Linda, *McCartney* was crafted by a single pair of hands. The album was given a very positive reception, and went straight to the top of the charts in the US; 1971's follow-up, *Ram*, was similarly successful.

In spite of controversy surrounding the banned "political" single "Give Ireland Back To The Irish", or "Hi Hi Hi", with its supposed drug references – also banned by the BBC – Paul's output has largely been characterized by lightweight catchy pop songs, often with trite lyrics. This may have been in stark contrast to John's cathartic soul-mining, but it found far greater favour with the public.

At the end of 1971, missing being part of a band, McCartney formed Wings. His sidemen were Denny Laine, an original member of the Moody Blues, and an unknown drummer, Denny Sewell. To the bemusement of the music world, Wings also featured Linda McCartney on keyboards. Press reaction to the band's debut album, *Wild Life*, was one of unprecedented hostility; *Red Rose Speedway*, attributed in 1973 to Paul McCartney and Wings, fared little better. The public, however, shared few of the media misgivings, both albums achieving healthy sales.

Paul's crowning achievement as a solo artist, *Band On The Run*, was released at the end of 1973. The album was recorded in Lagos, Nigeria, and featured a pair of million-selling singles – "Jet" and the album's epic title track. *Band On The Run* would spend over two years in the charts and, with world sales at the time exceeding six million, was one of the ten biggest-selling albums of the decade.

While McCartney's subsequent albums came nowhere near to matching the commercial success of *Band On The Run*, they still sold in large quantities. But even he surpassed himself, and The Beatles, with his 1977 single, "Mull of Kintyre". A pretty, if rather bland paean to his Scottish home, complete with the sounds of a 21-piece bagpipe band, it topped the UK charts for nine weeks. By the time it left the Top 30, it had sold 2.6 million copies, making it Britain's biggest-selling single to date and selling almost a million copies more than its nearest rival – "She Loves You" by The Beatles.

Since the 1980s, McCartney has continued to record and perform, often with great success, although it is now less regular or guaranteed. But a songwriter of Paul's pedigree – he has sold more records throughout the world than any other single artist – is always liable to pull off yet another masterstroke.

GEORGE HARRISON – DARK HORSE

George had already been the first Beatle with a solo release to his name. At the end of 1967 he had agreed to perform the soundtrack to his friend Joe

Below: George Harrison with members of a Hindu sect.

Opposite: George at London Airport, March 14, 1970.

Massot's experimental film *Wonderwall* (1968). But, after the breakup of The Beatles, it was George who surprisingly made the early running. In the middle of 1970, he assembled a star-studded band at Abbey Road under the keen eye of Phil Spector. The result was *All Things Must Pass*, an ambitious triple album boxed set. In early 1971, the song "My Sweet Lord" was lifted from the album for a single release. It was to be the biggest-selling hit of that year, both single and album topping the charts simultaneously on both sides of the Atlantic. Critics were full of praise – to them it showed that the high standard of his final Beatles contributions had been no fluke.

Harrison quickly followed with a further triumph. His long-time friend Ravi Shankar, appalled at the level of starvation in India, approached him with a view to organizing a benefit concert for UNICEF – the children's charity working under appalling conditions in Bangladesh. Shankar had an aim of raising $25,000. George threw himself headlong into the task, quickly organizing some of rock's top stars to perform a free benefit concert. All The Beatles were invited, causing a flurry of interest from the music press. Paul, fearing a new outbreak of "Beatles Reform" mania, refused to participate. John, who had agreed to begin with, also pulled out when it became clear that Yoko Ono was not to be one of the guest artists.

On August 1, 1971, two concerts were performed before an audience of 20,000 at Madison Square Garden in New York. The first was a raga specially written by Ravi Shankar. For many Westerners this piece would represent an introduction to the music of India. But it was the second concert that everyone had really come to see – George taking most of the vocal duties backed by a 25-piece band that featured among others: Ringo Starr, Bob Dylan, Eric Clapton, members of Badfinger, Leon Russell, Billy Preston and Klaus Voormann.

Royalties from the concerts raised nearly $250,000; the album and film that followed brought in a staggering total of $15 million. Eventually, thanks to the corporate greed of the various record companies involved, and the intervention of the IRS – the US tax authority – only a sm/all proportion of the money reached its destination, but Harrison and Shankar both received awards from the UNICEF organization for their efforts.

George's follow-up album, 1973's *Living In The*

Left: Maureen and Ringo on the way to the premiere of Ringo's film *The Magic Christian*, January 27, 1970.

Opposite: Elton John, Marc Bolan, Ringo Starr and Mickey Finn, December 15, 1973.

Material World, was also a major success, yielding another big hit single, "Give Me Love (Give Me Peace On Earth)". Thereafter, new releases would enjoy less critical acclaim and substantially lower sales.

In 1987, his profile was suddenly raised with the founding of the Traveling Wilburys – a supergroup to end all supergroups. With the combined talents of Harrison, Bob Dylan, Jeff Lynne (from the Electric Light Orchestra), Roy Orbison and Tom Petty, success was more or less guaranteed. However, the project's crowning achievement was to return Orbison – one of The Beatles' early heroes – to the forefront of the pop world before his death in December 1988.

For much of the 1990s, the ever-spiritual George seemed happy to live the life of a recluse, shut away in his country mansion, never over-exerting himself or over-eager to recapture former glories. However, his health began to fail toward the end of the decade, beginning in 1997 when he was treated for throat cancer. Two years later, he suffered a knife attack by an interloper claiming to be "on a mission from God" to kill him. George suffered seven stab wounds, a punctured lung and head injuries before the assailant was incapacitated by Olivia Harrison, his wife.

In 2001, the press revealed that George Harrison was being treated in the US for lung cancer, which quickly spread to his brain. He died on November 29, 2001 at the age of 58. As he had requested, his ashes were scattered in the River Ganges by his close family in a private ceremony in accordance with Hindu tradition.

RINGO STARR – EASY COME, EASY GO

During 1974, John Lennon claimed during an interview that the only reason The Beatles had stayed together after *The White Album* was because they were worried that Ringo wouldn't be able to do anything on his own. He then went on to remark with irony that over the past year, Ringo had probably outsold his own efforts. Based on Starr's regular stints behind the microphone with The Beatles, his flourishing mid-1970s solo career came as something of a surprise.

He had begun *Sentimental Journey*, his debut album, during 1969. Backed by George Martin's Orchestra, Ringo crooned a dozen standards from his childhood. Although not without charm, it illustrated – if anyone really needed to be told – that he was not one of the world's great balladeers. Predictably, Ringo's earliest albums were the weakest and least successful of all The Beatles' solo efforts. However, from 1972 he enjoyed a three-year run of hit singles, beginning with "It Don't Come Easy" and "Back off Boogaloo", which matched the success of his former colleagues and paved the way for a splendidly eccentric pop career.

Ringo's career hit its peak at the end of 1973. A highly-rated new single, "Photograph" written with George, topped the charts in the US, and its parent album, *Ringo*, was similarly successful. This album was of particular significance in that it is the closest The Beatles ever got to a full reunion. With an all-star line-up, *Ringo* featured not only his three esteemed colleagues, but Marc Bolan, members of The Band, Steve Cropper, Billy Preston, and a host of LA's top session men. A second single lifted from the album – a cover of

Johnny Burnette's "You're Sixteen" also topped the US singles chart. In all, *Ringo* sold over two million copies: by this time, of his former band mates, only Paul McCartney was outselling him.

Ringo was unable to match this success, and while he has continued to record and perform, both as a solo artist and with his celebrity-studded All-Starr Band, his commercial profile remains low – at least by Fab Four standards.

He also tried his luck in the movie business. In the first half of the 1970s he acted in a diverse selection of offbeat film roles: *Son of Dracula*, Frank Zappa's *2000 Motels*, Ken Russell's *Lisztomania*, and the spaghetti western *Blindman*. He also played to great acclaim the role of a Teddy Boy in *That'll Be The Day*. Ringo is probably best remembered by children growing up in the 1980s and 1990s as the narrator of classic TV series, *Thomas The Tank Engine*.

Even at the height of Beatlemania, Ringo had always enjoyed immense personal popularity, and although in interviews the Ringo of today can occasionally come across as an embittered man, he remains a bizarrely charismatic figure.

THE POPULARITY CONTINUES

Throughout the 1970s the music press with dull regularity would report rumours that The Beatles were about to reunite. They all played on the *Ringo* album – if not at the same time – but by the end of the decade, while three Beatle careers were on a downward trajectory, Paul was on top of the world:

there would have been little incentive for him to take part in a reunion. Of course, John's death on December 8, 1980 put an end to all such speculation.

Nonetheless, thanks to the wonders of technology, The Beatles *did* record together again. In 1994, work began on the *Anthology* series – a five-part television series and triple set of double-CDs. The audio component was especially interesting in that it provided a fascinating new insight into The Beatles story, containing out-takes or alternative versions to some of the most famous songs in the history of popular music. As part of the project, however, the three surviving Beatles agreed to produce two final new Beatles tracks, made possible by working on a pair of John's unfinished home demos from 1977.

The first effort, "Free As A Bird", was not even a complete song. Under the guidance of top producer Jeff Lynne, two of John's verses were transformed into a complete song. That and the second single, "Real Love",

Previous spread: Ringo Starr in London, 1973.

Above: Paul McCartney, Linda McCartney, Jimmy McCulloch, Denny Laine and Geoff Britton of Wings in 1974.

Opposite: Jeff Lynne and George Martin at *The Beatles Anthology* launch, London, November 15, 1995.

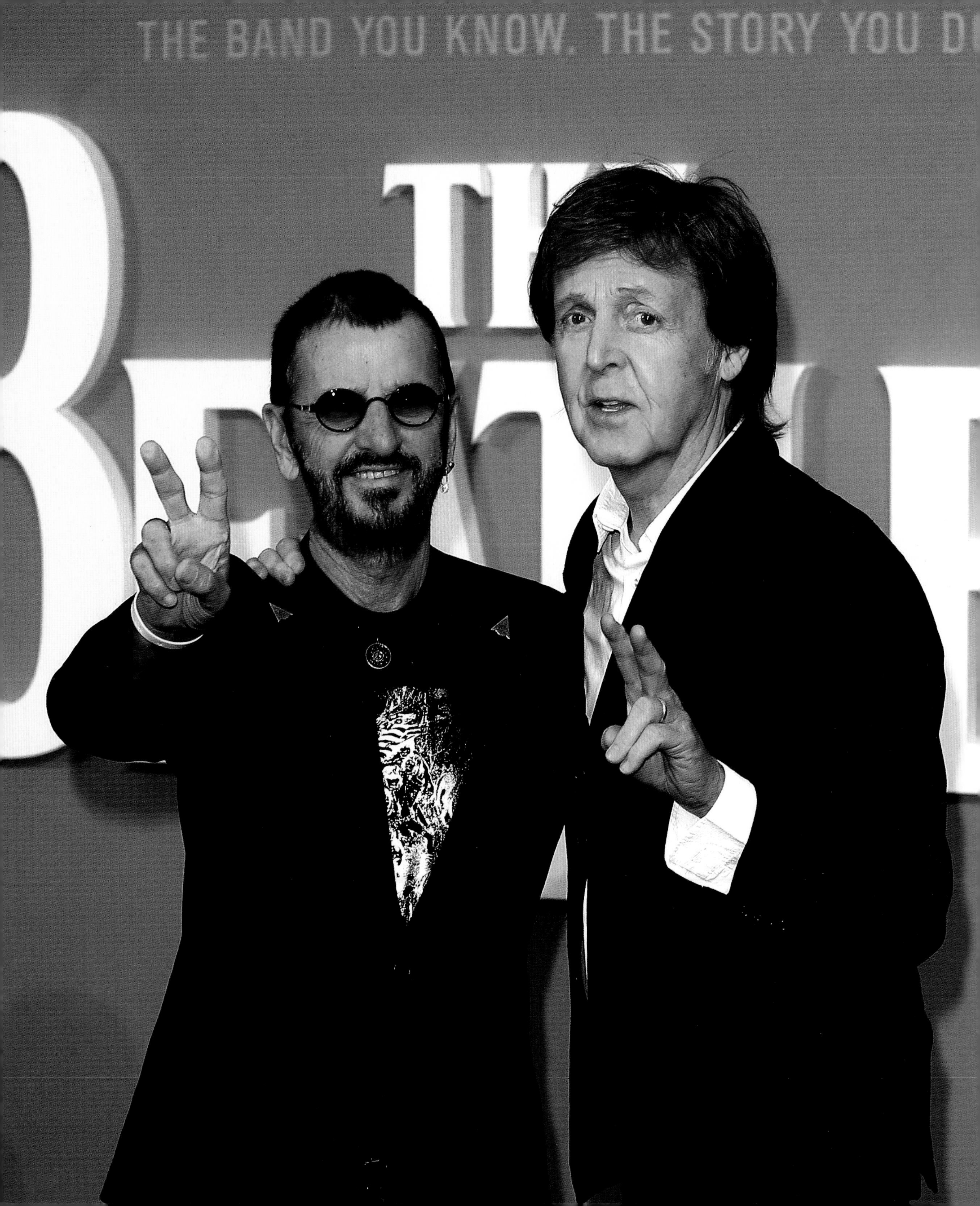
THE BAND YOU KNOW. THE STORY YOU D

broadly resembled The Beatles from the *Abbey Road/Let It Be* era.

The *Anthology* series and both singles sold in large quantities across the world proving that there was still an enormous demand for the Fab Four. And much of this renewed interest was coming from younger fans.

As the 21st century got underway, a brief new wave of Beatlemania hit as Apple released *1*, a compilation of every Beatles song to have topped the charts either in Britain or the US. Thirty years after the break-up of the band, The Beatles were still able to set new records: selling 12 million copies during the first three weeks of release, *1* became the fastest-selling album of all time.

The Beatles charted again two years later with the release of *Let It Be ... Naked*. Supervised by Paul, it was a "reconceived" version of the album restored to its earliest form, stripped of Spector's orchestral effects.

2006 saw the issue of a rather unlikely Beatles product. Using contemporary digital production techniques, *Love* is a "mash-up" collage incorporating segments of almost 30 Beatles classics. Produced by Martin and his producer son, Giles, it was created as a soundtrack to a show of the same name by Cirque du Soleil. Again, the album topped charts across the globe.

AND IN THE END...

When asked at the height of Beatlemania how long he thought The Beatles would last, John Lennon's reply was a cautious one: "You can be big-headed and say 'Yeah, we're gonna last ten years,' but as soon as you've said that you think ... we're lucky if we last three months." It's now over half a century since The Quarry Men played their first ramshackle skiffle concerts, and yet interest in The Beatles shows no sign of abating. The success of *1* , the hype surrounding the 2009 remastered editions and the band's first appearance on iTunes the following year illustrated The Beatles' enduring ability to cross the divides of taste and generation. In the years since their demise successive new generations of music fans have continued to buy into the legend of The Beatles. Their classic albums, from *Revolver* to *Abbey Road*, continue to sell in large numbers. If any greater proof were needed of their enduring appeal, *Rolling Stone Magazine* has a 500 Greatest Albums of All Time list: three of the top five are by The Beatles, including, in the No. 1 position, *Sgt. Pepper*. The majority of the magazine's readership would not even have been born when that album was recorded. Who would bet against a similar result 10, 25 or 50 years from now?

Opposite: Ringo and Paul at the world premiere of *The Beatles: Eight Days A Week – The Touring Years* in London, September 15, 2016.

Above: A statue of The Beatles adorns the wall outside Penny Lane Community Centre in Liverpool on February 11, 2016.

DISCOGRAPHY

	ORIGINAL UK ALBUMS		ORIGINAL UK SINGLES		ORIGINAL UK EPS
1962			05-10-62 Love Me Do / P.S. I Love You		
1963	22-03-63 *Please Please Me* 22-11-63 *With The Beatles*		11-01-63 Please Please Me / Ask Me Why 11-04-63 From Me To You / Thank You Girl 23-08-63 She Loves You / I'll Get You 29-11-63 I Want To Hold Your Hand / This Boy		12-07-63 Twist and Shout 06-09-63 The Beatles' Hits 01-11-63 The Beatles (No. 1)
1964	10-07-64 *A Hard Day's Night* 04-12-64 *Beatles For Sale*		20-03-64 Can't Buy Me Love / You Can't Do That 10-07-64 A Hard Day's Night / Things We Said Today 27-11-64 I Feel Fine / She's A Woman		07-02-64 All My Loving 19-06-64 Long Tall Sally 06-11-64 Extracts from the Film and Album *A Hard Day's Night* (x2)
1965	06-08-65 *Help!* 03-12-65 *Rubber Soul*		09-04-65 Ticket to Ride / Yes It Is 23-07-65 Help! / I'm Down 03-12-65 We Can Work It Out / Day Tripper		06-04-65 Beatles for Sale 04-06-65 Beatles for Sale (No. 2) 06-12-65 The Beatles' Million Sellers
1966	05-08-66 *Revolver*		10-06-66 Paperback Writer / Rain 05-08-66 Yellow Submarine / Eleanor Rigby		04-03-66 Yesterday 08-07-66 Nowhere Man
1967	01-06-67 *Sgt. Pepper's Lonely* *Hearts Club Band*		17-02-67 Strawberry Fields Forever / Penny Lane 07-07-67 All You Need Is Love / Baby You're a Rich Man 24-11-67 Hello Goodbye / I Am the Walrus		08-12-67 Magical Mystery Tour
1968	22-11-68 *The Beatles* *(The White Album)*		15-03-68 Lady Madonna / The Inner Light 30-08-68 Hey Jude / Revolution		
1969	17-01-69 *Yellow Submarine* 26-09-69 *Abbey Road*		11-04-69 Get Back / Don't Let Me Down 30-05-69 The Ballad of John and Yoko / Old Brown Shoe 31-10-69 Something / Come Together		
1970	08-05-70 *Let It Be*		06-03-70 Let It Be / You Know My Name 20-03-95 Baby It's You / I'll Follow the Sun Devil in Her Heart / Boys 12-12-95 Free as a Bird / I Saw Her Standing There This Boy / Christmas Time 04-03-96 Real Love / Baby's in Black Yellow Submarine / Here, There and Everywhere		

ORIGINAL US ALBUMS ## ORIGINAL US SINGLES

22-07-63	*Introducing... The Beatles*	25-02-63	Please Please Me / From Me To You	26-12-63	I Want To Hold Your Hand / I Saw Her	
		27-05-63	From Me To You / Thank You Girl		Standing There	
		16-09-63	She Loves You / I'll Get You			

20-01-64	*Meet The Beatles!*	30-01-64	Please Please Me / From Me To You	13-07-64	A Hard Day's Night / I Should Have
10-04-64	*The Beatles' Second Album*	08-02-64	All My Loving / This Boy		Known Better
26-06-64	*A Hard Day's Night*	02-03-64	Twist and Shout / There's a Place	20-07-64	I'll Cry Instead / Happy Just to Dance
20-07-64	*Something New*	16-03-64	Can't Buy Me Love / You Can't Do That		with You
15-12-64	*Beatles '65*	23-03-64	Do You Want to Know a Secret / Thank You Girl	20-07-64	And I Love Her / If I Fell
		27-04-64	Love Me Do / P.S. I Love You	24-08-64	Matchbox / Slow Down
		21-05-64	Sie Liebt Dich / I'll Get You	23-11-64	I'm Fine / She's A Woman

22-03-65	*The Early Beatles*	15-02-65	Eight Days a Week / Don't Want to	13-09-65	Yesterday / Act Naturally
14-06-65	*Beatles VI*		Spoil the Party	06-12-65	We Can Work it Out / Day Tripper
13-08-65	*Help!*	19-07-65	Help! / I'm Down		
06-12-65	*Rubber Soul*				

06-06-66	*Yesterday... and Today*	21-02-66	Nowhere Man / What Goes On
08-08-66	*Revolver*	30-05-66	Paperback Writer / Rain
		08-08-66	Yellow Submarine / Eleanor Rigby

02-06-67	*Sgt. Pepper's Lonely*	13-02-67	Penny Lane / Strawberry Fields Forever
	Hearts Club Band	17-07-67	All You Need Is Love / Baby You're a
27-11-67	*Magical Mystery Tour*		Rich Man
		27-11-67	Hello Goodbye / I Am the Walrus

25-11-68	*The Beatles*	18-03-68	Lady Madonna / The Inner Light
	(The White Album)	05-05-68	Get Back / Don't Let Me Down
		26-08-68	Hey Jude / Revolution

13-01-69	*Yellow Submarine*	04-06-69	The Ballad of John and Yoko /
01-10-69	*Abbey Road*		Old Brown Shoe
		06-10-69	Come Together / Something

		11-03-70	Let It Be / You Know My Name
		11-05-70	The Long and Winding Road / For You Blue
		31-05-76	Got to Get You Into My Life / Helter Skelter
26-02-70	*Hey Jude*	08-06-76	Ob-La-Di, Ob-La-Da / Julia
18-05-70	*Let It Be*	17-04-95	Baby It's You / I'll Follow the Sun / Devil in
			Her Heart / Boys
		12-12-95	Free as a Bird / Christmas Time
		04-03-96	Real Love / Baby's in Black

UK COMPILATION ALBUMS

09-12-66	*A Collection of Beatles Oldies*
	Parlophone Records
19-04-73	*1962–1966 (The Red Album)*
19-04-73	*1967–1970 (The Blue Album)*
07-06-76	*Rock 'N' Roll Music*
19-11-76	*Magical Mystery Tour*
04-05-77	*The Beatles At The Hollywood Bowl*
19-11-77	*Love Songs*
02-11-78	*The Beatles Collection*
02-12-78	*Rarities*
14-10-80	*Beatles Ballads*
23-03-82	*Reel Music*
11-10-82	*20 Greatest Hits*
07-03-88	*Past Masters, Volume One*
07-03-88	*Past Masters, Volume Two*
15-11-88	*The Beatles Box Set*
30-11-94	*Live at the BBC*
21-11-95	*Anthology 1*
18-03-96	*Anthology 2*
28-10-96	*Anthology 3*
13-09-99	*Submarine Songtrack*
13-11-00	*The Beatles 1*
17-11-03	*Let It Be... Naked*
16-11-04	*The Capitol Albums, Volume 1*
11-04-06	*The Capitol Albums, Volume 2*
20-11-06	*Love*
09-09-09	*The Beatles in Mono*
09-09-09	*The Beatles Stereo Box Set*

INDEX

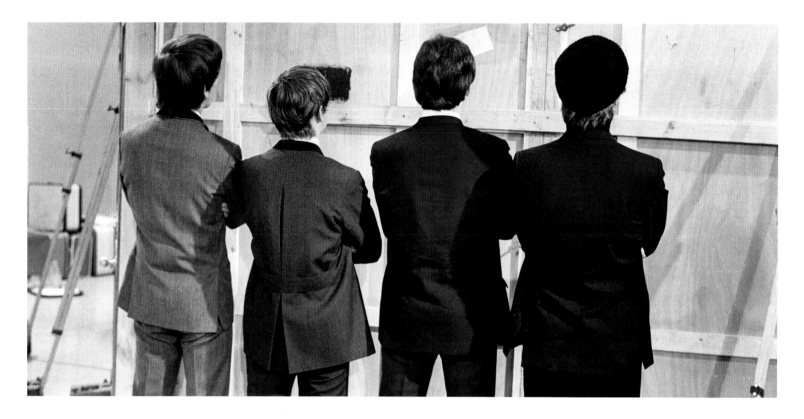

PICTURE CREDITS

The publishers would like to thank the following sources for their kind permission to reproduce the pictures in this book.